Basic Wiring for Model Railroaders

The Complete Photo Guide

— SECOND EDITION —

Rick Selby

KALMBACH
BOOKS

Printed in the United States of America

11 10 09 08 07   1 2 3 4 5

Visit our Web site at
kalmbachbooks.com
Secure online ordering available

Publisher's Cataloging-In-Publication Data
(Prepared by The Donohue Group, Inc.)

Selby, Rick.
   Basic wiring for model railroaders : the complete photo guide / Rick Selby. --2nd ed.

   p. : ill. ; cm.

   ISBN: 978-0-89024-655-9

1. Railroads--Models--Electric equipment. 2. Digital control systems. I. Title.

TF197 .S423 2007
625.1/9

About the author

As a teenager, Rick Selby worked in a San Jose, California, hobby shop, where he began acquiring his knowledge of model railroading. Then, as a columnist for *Model Railroader*'s Student Fare department, Rick enthusiastically shared his knowledge with an audience of student-age, typically entry-level model railroaders. His ability to clarify some of the more confusing aspects of model railroading made him an ideal author for his first Kalmbach book, *HO Railroad from Set to Scenery*, and for the 2nd edition of this entry-level book.

Rick now works as a game designer in Redmond, Washington. He is an NMRA member and has been an active model railroader for more than 30 years. When he's not building models, Rick also enjoys railfanning, photography, automobiles, and golf.

Contents

Basic electrical know-

how

Many new hobbyists look at some model railroads and assume they'll need an electrical engineering degree to wire their own layout. But electrical wiring does not have to be a difficult task. In fact, you don't need to know much at all about electrical theory to get your trains up and running. Some basic information and a little common sense provides everything you need for doing it right.

This book is not intended to be a definitive source on the nuances of electrical theory. However, you will encounter a few electronic terms as you examine your power pack and other electrical components.

You will find it helpful to be familiar with these terms as you begin any wiring project for two-rail, DC-powered trains. Let's take a quick look at these terms and what they mean.

Voltage and current

Electricity has two basic components: voltage and current. These two components work together to define the characteristics of an electrical circuit. To better understand these two concepts, let's use the analogy of a spinning lawn sprinkler attached to a garden hose.

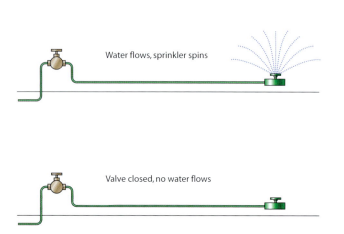

Water flows, sprinkler spins

Valve closed, no water flows

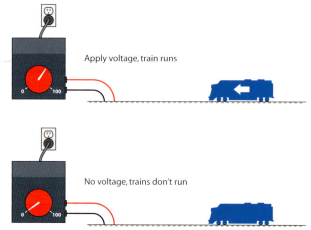

Apply voltage, train runs

No voltage, trains don't run

Turn on the water. In our analogy, voltage is similar to the water pressure in the garden hose. When you close the faucet valve, you prevent water flow to the garden hose, but water pressure still exists inside the pipe upstream from the valve. When you open the faucet valve, or complete the conductive path, water flows down the hose to the sprinkler. The sprinkler spins and waters the lawn. Pretty simple, right?

Turn on the train. Now let's apply this principle to electricity. Consider the voltage source coming out of your train's power pack. To run the train, you open the throttle to apply voltage to the electrical circuit for your layout, which includes the feeder wires, track, and locomotive motor. When the electrical path to the motor is interrupted – you close the throttle or disconnect a wire – no electricity flows, and your train does not run.

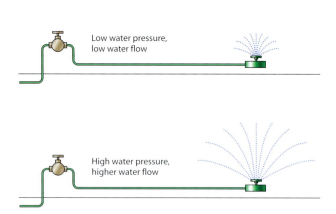

Low water pressure, low water flow

High water pressure, higher water flow

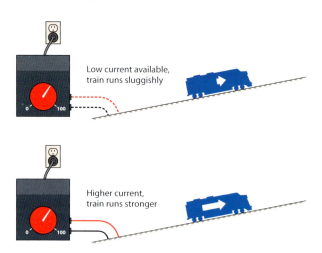

Low current available, train runs sluggishly

Higher current, train runs stronger

The spin on current. Now let's continue the analogy to define electrical current. Using the garden hose example, if you open the faucet a quarter turn or so, only a small amount of water flows to the sprinkler, and it spins slowly. However, if you open the faucet all the way, a lot of water flows to the sprinkler and it spins much faster. Of course, there is a limit – if you want to water your lawn at a rate of 5 gallons per minute, you need to push the water through the hose with more pressure than if you only needed 2 gallons a minute. But at some point, your hose and faucet – your water circuit – reaches its maximum gallons-per-minute capacity.

The driving force. The amount of water flowing through a hose is comparable to the amount of electrical current flowing through a circuit. Electrical current is what drives the motor in your locomotive and gives your train the oomph it needs to climb a grade. Just as a garden hose with little water pressure barely spins the lawn sprinkler, an electrical circuit of the proper voltage, but without sufficient current, will cause locomotive motors under load to run sluggishly or not at all. As a result, your wiring and power supply have to be up to the task of powering the load you place on them. Electrical current is typically measured in units called amperes, or amps.

AC and DC

For our purposes, the last important characteristic of electricity is the distinction between direct current and alternating current. The different types of current have unique characteristics, and each type has a use in model railroading.

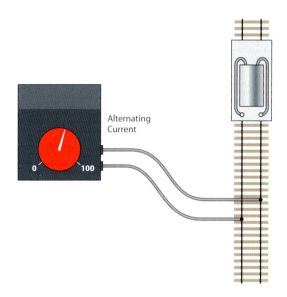

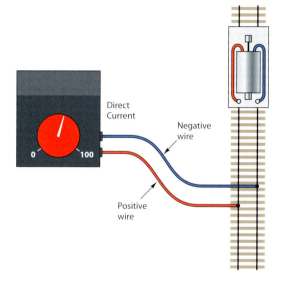

Back and forth. With alternating current (AC), the electrons continually change direction as the wire is energized. This means that neither wire has a constant polarity. Some model trains, such as Lionel O-27 sets, Märklin HO trains, and some other European models, operate on alternating current. Many accessories for all types of trains, such as automatic switch machines, also operate on AC. AC accessories are covered in chapter 7.

One way. With direct current (DC), the electrons that constitute electricity flow at the speed of light from the power pack transformer, down one feeder wire to one rail, through the motor, back through the other rail and feeder wire, and to the transformer to complete the electrical circuit. This flow moves in one direction and leaves one feeder wire/rail pair positively charged (+) and the other negatively charged (-). This electrical charge is referred to as polarity – one wire has a positive polarity, the other a negative polarity. Most HO, N, and G scale model trains run on direct current.

Putting it all together

Now that you're familiar with the basic concepts, let's put it all together and look at a typical model railroad environment. A typical N or HO scale locomotive runs on a 12-volt DC circuit and draws less than 0.5 amp of current under full load. A typical G scale locomotive runs on 18 volts and draws less than 1 amp of current. Both of these circuits are considered to be low-voltage compared to the typical 110-volt, 15-amp circuit available in the wall socket of your home. This low-voltage, low-current circuit can cause a mild electrical shock, but it won't cause any physical harm.

The relatively high voltage circuit in the wall socket, however, can cause injury or death. That's why our trains run on low voltage. The transformer takes the 110-volt electricity from the wall and steps it down to the 12 or 18 volts needed to run a model train. The throttle control varies the voltage to the rails, changing the speed of the motor and, consequently, the rate your locomotive moves down the track.

No matter how complex a layout you plan to build, the basic principle behind model train control is the same – you control train speed and direction by varying the voltage and polarity of the electricity reaching the motor. From a simple loop of track to a basement empire or a garden railway, all train operation follows this same basic principle.

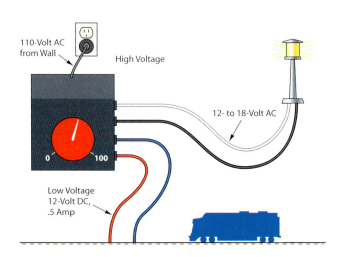

110-Volt AC from Wall

High Voltage

12- to 18-Volt AC

Low Voltage 12-Volt DC, .5 Amp

With this concept in mind, you need a few basic components to make your model railroad run. At the most basic level, you need a power pack, track, feeder wires, and a locomotive.

There are many different options out there, but generally speaking, they all work the same. Let's look at each of these components in more detail.

Power packs come in all shapes and sizes. The type of unit you need depends on the layout you plan to build. Small layouts can get by with a basic unit like those found in many starter train sets. Larger layouts or those with lots of accessories will require power packs with a greater power output. You can upgrade your power pack as your layout grows and use your older units to power accessories and turnouts.

All power packs contain a transformer to provide the 12 volts, a throttle to vary the output voltage, and a direction switch to control the polarity of the circuit. Power packs also have screw terminals for DC track and AC accessory connections. More elaborate units may feature a larger power supply; additional electronic features such as operating modes, pilot lights, and meters; and multiple terminals for accessories including add-on walkaround throttle units.

Model railroad locomotives collect electrical current from the metal rails as their metal wheels ride on the rails. The electricity is routed from the wheels to the motor, which connects to the wheels through a mechanical drive system. When the electricity turns the motor, the motor turns the wheels, and the train runs. Regardless of scale, all model locomotives operate the same way.

The contact point where a locomotive's wheels meet the rail is extremely small, as this photo of an HO scale locomotive truck shows. Consequently, it doesn't take much in the way of dust, dirt, or debris to obstruct wheel-to-rail contact. It is important that you keep the wheels clean and free of accumulated dirt. If the wheels become dirty, they may not make good contact with the metal rails, and your train will stall.

Locomotives from different manufacturers use different electrical designs. A Walthers/Life-Like HO scale Proto-2000 diesel (left) uses wires to carry electricity from the wheels to the motor, which is encased in a cast-metal weight. Kato HO scale locomotives (center) use wires to carry electricity from the trucks to an electrical connector on top of the motor. Athearn's newer HO scale models (right) feature wires that connect to a main circuit board on top of the motor. The locomotive's lights also attach to this circuit board assembly. Both the Proto-2000 and Athearn locomotive are DCC-ready, meaning that they can accept a Digital Command Control decoder, which is examined in chapter 6.

Model railroad track is very simple in design. Track consists of two metal rails separated by plastic tie sections. Each rail carries one side of the electrical circuit. It is important that these two rails do not contact each other, or that a metal object does not contact both rails simultaneously, as this will cause a short circuit that could damage your power pack if it happens repeatedly or for a long period of time.

Cleaning track

Over time, your track accumulates dust and debris. As your train runs around, this dust collects and compacts on the wheels and rails, forming a nonconductive film. As this layer of material accumulates, it interrupts electrical contact and causes your locomotive to run poorly or stop altogether.

The solution to this problem is easy. Simply remove the layer of dirt from your locomotive wheels and rails, and railroad operation returns to normal. There are several effective techniques for removing dirt from track.

Abrasive track-cleaning blocks are one of the simplest and cheapest ways to clean track. To use an abrasive track block, simply rub the tops of the rails with the block. As you scrub the rails, the accumulated dirt transfers to the abrasive block. Use care when cleaning track with an abrasive block, so you do not damage lineside details such as telephone poles and signals.

Track-cleaning fluid works to restore electrical contact to your track. Products like Rail-Zip promote electrical contact and work to prevent oxidation and dirt build-up. To use these products, you apply them to the rail on a regular basis while running the train. You can wipe the rails down if they become heavily soiled.

Doug Nighswonger's Milwaukee Road Layout

When you assemble your track and connect the power pack, you're ready to start running trains. Plug in the power pack, place the locomotive on the track, turn up the throttle, and you're ready to go. The details of wiring a basic train set start in Chapter 3.

Use caution

Use care with track-cleaning fluid. Some brands are flammable, so do not use the product around an open flame. Fumes can also be toxic, so always provide adequate ventilation. Keep all track-cleaning fluids away from young children.

Isopropyl alcohol also works as a track cleaner. It acts as a solvent to break down and remove the dirt layer. To use, dampen a towel and wipe the top of the rail heads. Switch to a new section of the towel as it becomes soiled with dirt.

Track-cleaning cars are easy to use – simply place the car in the consist of your train and operate your layout as you normally do. As the train runs, the track-cleaning car scrubs the rails using an abrasive pad. This prevents the accumulation of dust and debris.

Tools and supplies

CHAPTER 2

While the thought of wiring a model railroad can be daunting, the right tools and supplies go a long way toward making the job easier.

Before you start your wiring project, make sure your toolbox contains the items you'll need to complete the job. If you start a project and then find you're missing a tool, progress stops until you return from that unplanned trip to the hardware store. The tool list here covers the basics, but there are additional tools you might find useful as you browse through the hardware store.

Let's start with the tools you need in your model railroading toolbox.

Tools

Wire cutters are essential even for the most basic wiring jobs. Diagonal-cut models, like those shown here, are most common. Wire cutters also come in flush-cut models, which work for wire, metal stock, and track. Flush-cut models tend to make a cleaner cut, but they also cost a little more. For basic jobs, either type will work. In fact, you'll find that both types come in handy, so if your budget permits, purchase one of each.

To cut wire, place the wire between the blades and squeeze the handle. The wire end should cut cleanly and fall away from the tool. Be sure to check and double-check the length of the wire you are cutting. Extra care here avoids wasted materials.

Wire strippers remove the insulation from the wire conductor. Standard models are capable of removing wire insulation from wire gauges 8 to 22 and are perfect for most model railroad applications.

Stripping a wire is easy with this tool. Insert the wire end into the notch in the tool that corresponds to the wire size. Then squeeze the handle. The tool clamps the wire, cuts the insulation, and removes it from the metal conductor, leaving a bare wire end. Afterward, release the handle and remove the wire from the tool.

Electrical tape is readily available at hardware and electronic supply stores. Always insulate wire connections with electrical tape to prevent the bare conductor from contacting another wire and causing a short circuit.

To use electrical tape, attach the end to the wire joint and then wrap the tape tightly around the joint, unrolling the tape as you go. The tape should stretch tightly around the wire joint. Apply tape until you cover all exposed metal. Remember, any bare metal is a potential source of trouble.

A range of small screwdrivers, both Phillips and flathead, come in handy for securing wires to terminal strips and contact posts on power supplies and other electronic devices.

Needlenose pliers are handy for all sorts of chores. You use them to twist wire ends together for soldering or to hold wires in place while fastening terminal screws.

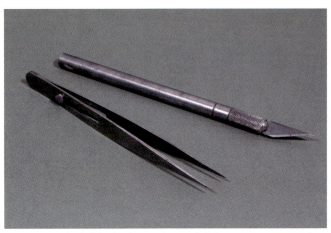

Tweezers and a hobby knife are also useful. The tweezers can help position wires on terminals and along track rail when soldering feeder wires, and the knife is useful for trimming wire insulation.

Electrical test meters are useful for testing and troubleshooting layout wiring. Test meters come in many configurations and prices, but a simple, inexpensive analog meter can serve the needs of most model railroaders. A digital meter costs a bit more, but it is more accurate and easier to use. Meters are available at most hardware and electronic supply stores.

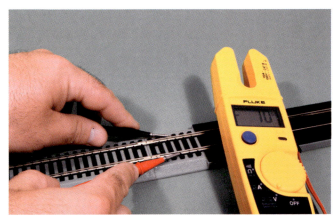

To test a circuit, place the meter probes on the rails or wires of the circuit you want to test. If voltage is flowing to the circuit, the meter shows a reading.

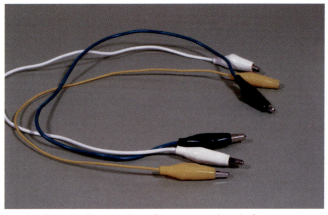

Test leads with alligator clips often come in handy for testing circuits so keep a few in your toolbox.

Working with wire

Wire comes in a large variety of sizes, types, and colors. Some types work well for model railroad applications and some don't.

Often, modelers are tempted to use wire that's inappropriate for their application. Many a modeler has built a layout using inexpensive multiple-conductor telephone cable, only to experience problems later on. This wire's small size makes it less than ideal for model railroad use.

Appropriately sized wire is not necessarily expensive if purchased in bulk at home improvement stores or electronic supply companies. Shop around to get the best deal on the wire you need, and don't be tempted to use the wrong wire even if the price seems right.

Electrical wire comes in two forms: solid-conductor and stranded-conductor. Both types can be useful for wiring model railroads. Solid wire uses a conductor that is made up of one solid piece of metal. Stranded wire is comprised of many smaller wire strands that, for a given wire size, equal the electrical capacity of the solid-conductor's larger strand.

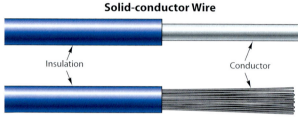

Solid-conductor Wire

Insulation   Conductor

Stranded-conductor Wire

Electrical wire has two basic components: the conductor and insulation. The conductor is the metal core that carries the electricity. This conductor is typically made of copper, which works well with the low current requirements in model railroad applications.

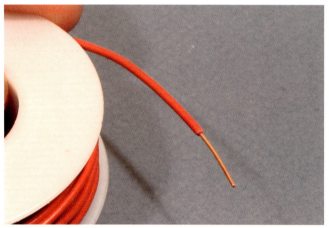

This is solid-conductor wire. The solid conductor makes it easy to connect this wire to terminal screws and connectors. However, solid-conductor wire is generally less flexible than stranded wire and, therefore, can be slightly more awkward to work with in tight spaces.

This is stranded-conductor wire. Stranded wire is flexible and easy to route underneath the benchwork. However, attaching it to screw terminals to keep the strands from fraying requires some extra effort.

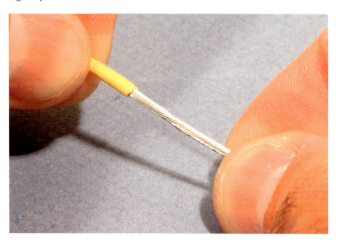

When attaching stranded wire to screw terminals or other connectors, twist the exposed conductor strands with your fingers to wrap them together. This helps keep them from fraying or breaking when you tighten the terminal screw.

Wire gauge

The size of a wire is referred to as its gauge. The specific gauge measurements refer to the actual size of the diameter of the wire conductor and are defined by the American Wire Gauge standards. As a rule, smaller numbers identify heavier wire, and larger numbers denote lighter wire.

Wire comes in all sorts of sizes. Larger wires, such as gauges 10 to 12, are capable of carrying high electrical current and are commonly used for 110-volt household wiring. Since model railroads operate on 12 volts at relatively low current ratings, you can use smaller wire. Wire between 18 and 22 gauge is the most useful for model railroad applications. There is some limited use for 14 or 16 gauge. Generally, 24 gauge wire is useful for connecting lights and other low-current accessories. Do not use anything smaller than 20 gauge wire to connect your track.

Wire gauge and typical uses

Wire gauge	Typical use
24 and smaller	Lights, other low-current accessories
22	Turnout machine feeders
18-20	Track feeders
14-16	Track power bus
12 and larger	110/220-volt household wiring – no practical model railroading use

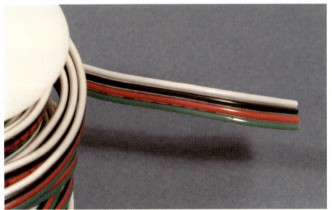

Multiple-conductor wire consists of two or more conductors connected with common insulation. The insulation on each strand is typically color-coded to help distinguish the wires from each other. Some multiple-conductor wires are wrapped in an outer sheathing to form a cable, while others are molded with the conductors running side by side, ribbon style. Functionally, they both work the same.

To use multiple-conductor wire, separate the individual wires and then strip the insulation from each conductor. Connect each wire in normal fashion. This wire comes in handy for wiring switch machines or other devices that require multiple connections.

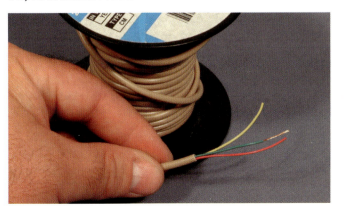

Cable wire is useful for switch machines and accessories. When working with cable wire, use a hobby knife to remove the outer sheathing, then strip the insulation from each wire. Use care when cutting the outer sheathing to avoid nicking the individual wire insulation. If you nick the insulation, you run the risk of a short circuit in the wire bundle, one that's extremely difficult to trace. Examine the wires carefully. If you notice nicks in the insulation, cut the wire end off and repeat the process.

Soldering

Despite the assortment of mechanical fasteners on the market, the best way to permanently join two wires together is with solder. When you solder wires, you melt a combination of tin and lead that adheres to bare metal. As the solder cools, it solidifies and securely joins the metal surfaces. It also forms an electrically continuous path, providing reliable connections. Soldering is easy if you follow a few basic guidelines and are careful. Inhaling solder fumes can cause irritation and other health problems. Let's look at the equipment you need and the basic techniques for soldering wires and track.

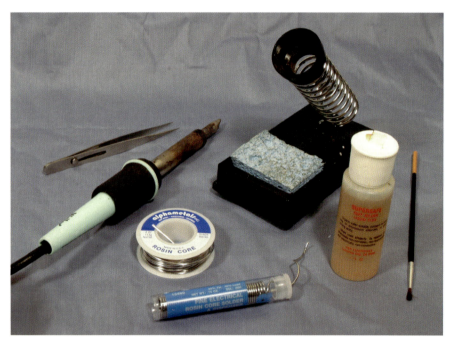

A standard soldering iron works for almost all model railroad needs. A 25-watt model is adequate for light wires, but if you intend to solder track or wires heavier than 14 gauge, purchase a 40- or 60-watt model.

You need several items to solder wires and track effectively. Almost all of these items are available at your local electronics supply or home improvement stores.

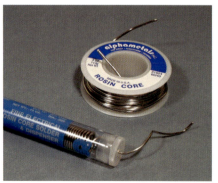

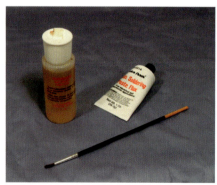

A soldering stand provides a convenient location to place the soldering iron when it's not in use. Use a stand that is sturdy and does not have a propensity to tip over. Many soldering iron stands also contain a well for a damp sponge, which comes in handy for cleaning accumulated solder and flux from the tip of the iron.

Solder comes in several varieties, but 60 percent tin/40 percent lead mixtures work well for model railroading needs. Several manufactures offer lead-free solder; since repeated exposure to lead can be poisonous, these solders have obvious health benefits. Use rosin-core solder for all your soldering activities. The rosin melts with the solder and helps conduct heat from the iron to the joint. Do not use acid-core solder, as it's not designed for electrical use, and over time it will cause metal corrosion.

Flux is a chemical that rapidly transfers heat from the iron to the joint, making the solder flow quickly. Flux comes in two forms, liquid or paste. Liquid flux is less messy to use. Apply it using a brush applicator, which is sometimes included in the bottle cap, depending on brand. Paste flux is sometimes easier to use, since it sticks to vertical joints and other awkward shapes. Apply paste flux using a brush, toothpick, or cotton swab.

Soldering wires

Let's look at the steps for soldering wires. First, twist the two wire ends together so the metal conductors contact each other. Make sure the wires are securely fastened together to prevent them from separating during soldering. Use tape, tweezers, or a pair of needlenose pliers to hold the wires in place if necessary. Use care to keep your hands well clear of the wire to prevent burns.

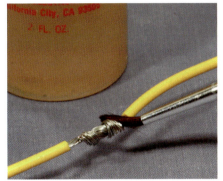

1. Apply a little flux to the wires using a cotton swab, toothpick, paintbrush, or similar instrument; don't use too much. Use care when handling flux, since it can be harmful to your skin and eyes.

2. You tin the soldering iron by coating it with solder. This helps transfer heat to the joint quickly, allowing clean, quick solder joints. Keep the tip of your iron clean. Regularly wipe the tip on a damp sponge to remove excess solder and burned flux, then re-apply a small amount of solder to the tip.

3. Touch the soldering iron tip to the wires to apply heat. As the iron contacts the wires, the flux boils and transfers the heat to the wire. A second or two is all it should take. Don't overheat the wires, or you might melt the wire insulation.

4. When the joint heats up, apply solder directly to the wires. As you touch the solder to the wire, it melts and flows over the joint. Touch the end of the solder to the wires themselves, not the soldering iron. This helps the solder flow to the wires instead of the iron. Apply solder until the conductors are adequately covered. Don't over-apply the solder, or it will drip from the joint and cause burns or damage to surfaces below.

5. Remove the soldering iron after solder flows over the entire joint. The solder joint will cool and harden a few seconds after you remove the iron. As the solder cools, its appearance changes from shiny to dull. After the solder joint cools, you can trim excess length from the solder wire connection if necessary using a pair of wire cutters. Gently tug on the wires to ensure they are firmly soldered together.

6. Always use electrical tape or shrink tubing to insulate the wire joints. This prevents short circuits. Time spent insulating wire connections will make troubleshooting much easier or eliminate potential problems all together.

Soldering track

In addition to wires, you can solder track sections together. Traditional rail joiners are notorious for working loose over time, causing intermittent contact problems and poor operation. Soldering track joints provides an electrically continuous path between track sections.

Soldering track requires extra work, but it provides a much more secure electrical path between your throttle and locomotive. And with a little practice, you can quickly master the technique.

One word of warning – do not solder track sections together if you plan to rearrange them later. Once track sections are soldered, they are difficult if not impossible to separate. Make sure you are happy with your track arrangement before soldering your track together.

And while this technique works well for both sectional and flextrack, it is not recommended for roadbed track. The mechanical fasteners built into this track design generally make soldered joints unnecessary.

1. Align the track sections straight and square. Apply the flux to the rail joint using a small brush. Cover the entire rail joint in flux, but don't apply too much.

2. Apply heat to the outside edge of the rail with the soldering iron. As the flux boils, apply solder to the outside edge of the rail joint. As the solder touches the joint, it flows through the rail joiner and bonds the track sections together.

3. Use care to not apply too much solder, since it can foul the inside rail edge and cause operational problems. Excess heat can melt the tie castings as the rails transfer heat to the plastic, so make your solder joints as quickly as possible.

Soldering feeder wires

You can use the same techniques to solder feeder wires directly to the rails. In many ways, this method is preferred to traditional feeder track sections or feeder rail joiners because it allows more flexibility in feeder wire placement. It's a useful technique when you need to apply a new feeder wire to a track section and can't easily remove the track sections because of track fasteners or ballast.

When soldering feeder wires directly to the rails, always install them on the outside edge of the rail. Feeders soldered to the inside edge of rails can interfere with passing train wheels and cause derailments.

Use caution when soldering wires or track. A wire joint will retain heat from the soldering iron for several minutes after completing the joint. Soldering irons get hot enough to cause severe burns, so use care when handling recently soldered wires or track.

1. Use a file to clean up the solder joint after it cools. The rail top and inside rail surfaces should be smooth from one section to the next; excess solder can cause derailments or other operational problems. Solder is a soft metal, so it only takes a few seconds to clean off excess solder from rail joints. Run your finger along the joint to check for burrs and bumps.

2. Drill a hole next to the rail for the feeder wire. Run the feeder up through the hole, strip the insulation, and bend the conductor to rest alongside the rail. Use a pair of needlenose pliers to hold the feeder against the rail. Bend the wire to sit alongside the outside edge of the rail. Apply flux to the rail and feeder wire. Don't apply too much.

3. Apply heat to the joint with the soldering iron. As the flux boils, apply solder to the joint. Use care so that you do not apply too much solder, and work quickly so you don't melt ties with the soldering iron.

4. Let the joint cool, then clean up the feeder connection as necessary. Use a small file to remove excess solder.

Wiring a basic train set

CHAPTER 3

Most model railroaders enter the hobby with a train set. Prepackaged sets come in scales from Z through G and are available at hobby shops and toy stores around the country. As a result, first-time modelers often see these sets as an easy way to get started, regardless of the scale they choose.

However, a person's future in the model railroading hobby is often determined by his or her success with this first train set. Many potential modelers are discouraged soon after their purchase because they can't make their set work reliably.

Setup and connection of a train set isn't difficult as long as you follow a few important steps. While the sets themselves vary, you use the same techniques to set them up and make them work, regardless of scale. Let's look at the steps you use to assemble and wire a basic train set.

Train set assembly

Beginning modelers basically have two choices when purchasing a train set: prepackaged sets and piece-together sets. Prepackaged sets typically include a locomotive, several freight cars, an oval or circle of track, a power pack, and hookup wire. If you want to select your own trains and track, ask your local hobby shop staff to suggest a piece-together train set alternative.

Many sets today include molded roadbed track, while others use traditional snap track pieces. These two types of track function the same way, but they are not compatible with each other. When purchasing additional track sections, you must buy the same kind of track (roadbed or snap-track) that was included with your set.

Electrical connections between track sections rely upon small metal contacts or rail joiners. If these contacts become dirty, loose or damaged, electricity might not flow reliably from section to section. This may cause the train to slow down on portions of the layout or stop altogether.

When assembling the sections, use care to ensure that you insert the rails properly into the rail joiners. Also, be sure to join the track sections tightly and align the sections squarely. If you damage a rail joiner or section of track, replace it with a new one.

Set the contents from the train set out on a table. Study the items to make sure that you have everything and that you know where each piece goes. Then read the instructions and electrical precautions thoroughly before you begin to assemble the track sections. Most sets are designed for easy assembly, so if you follow the instructions, you should have things up and running in a matter of minutes.

Track assembly

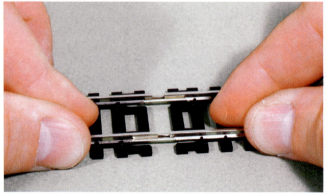

To assemble sectional track sections, use rail joiners for alignment and electrical connectivity. Hold the track sections in your hand, align the rail joiners, and then gently slide the track sections together. Make sure the sections join tightly, and use care not to damage or bend the rail joiners.

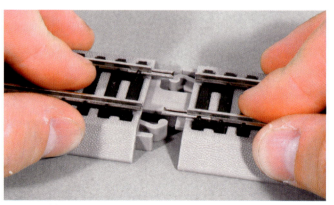

To assemble roadbed track sections, use fasteners underneath to help hold the track sections together. Place the pieces on your layout tabletop. Align the rail joiners so that they slide into place on the opposing section. Gently press the track sections together until the mechanical fasteners lock the track pieces together.

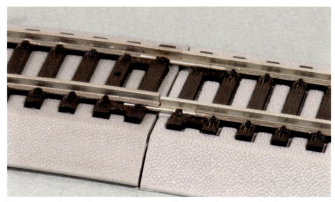

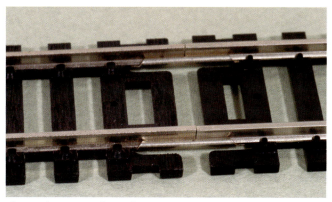

These track sections are not joined correctly. Note the large gaps between the rails and the slight kink in the track alignment where the sections meet. This condition causes poor electrical contact between track sections and can be a prime location for derailments.

With roadbed track, it is easy to misalign a rail joiner when assembling the track, as shown here. The sections will feel like they are securely fastened together, but one of the rails is not aligned properly. Be sure to check the rail joiners to ensure the track is assembled correctly.

The track sections shown here are joined securely. Note the lack of gaps between the rail ends and the square alignment of the track sections. For reliable operation, you want your track joints to look just like this.

Terminal track sections

The terminal track is where you connect the wires from the power pack to the track. There are several types of terminal tracks, but they all function the same electrically. Terminal track sections come in both curved and straight configurations and are designed to replace a standard length of sectional track. Starter sets usually include a terminal section as part of the track oval or circle.

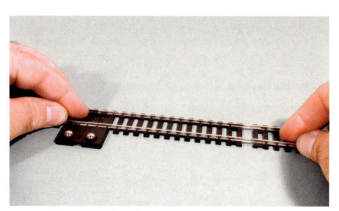

To install the terminal track section, select its position based on where you want to place the power pack. This straight terminal section replaces a standard straight section of track. Install it in the layout just as you would a normal track section.

Train set wiring

Feeder wires

Feeder wires deliver electricity to your track. A secure connection at each end of these wires helps guarantee trouble-free operation.

It does not really matter which wire you connect to what screw, but the position of these wires does affect the direction your train runs. For example, when you switch the wires at the terminal track, it reverses the polarity of the voltage going to the rails. Switching these wires has the same effect as moving the direction switch on a power pack.

If your train direction does not match the direction switch on your power pack, switch the leads at the screw connections on the power pack or the terminal track.

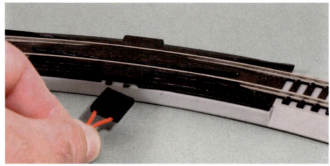

To connect feeder wires to roadbed track, simply plug the connector into the track section. This Bachmann track allows you to insert the plug on either side of the terminal track, depending upon the placement of your power pack; pick the side that is most convenient for your particular layout. Place the power pack close to the terminal track section so you don't have to lengthen the leads with additional wire.

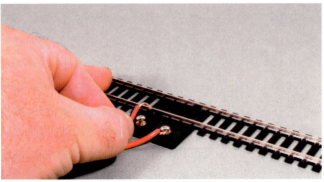

1. To attach the feeders to a terminal track with screws, strip the wire insulation from the power pack leads using wire strippers. Solid wire works best here, but you can use stranded wire as well. Loosen the screws and wrap the wires clockwise around the screw threads so they pull against the screw threads when you tighten the connection.

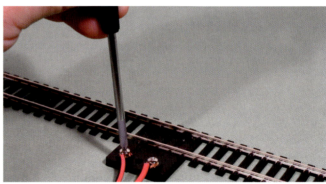

2. Tighten the terminal track screws to secure the wires. As you tighten the screw, the wire snugs up against the screw threads, providing a secure electrical connection. Do not overtighten the terminal screws, or you may break or crush the wire conductor.

3. Attach the other end of the wires to the terminal screws on the power pack. If necessary, strip the wire insulation from the ends of the wires, then bend the wire conductor in a hook shape and place it clockwise around the screw. Alternatively, you can use spade connectors as shown here. Connect the track feeders to the terminals marked "track," "trains," or "DC." Do not attach the wires to "AC" or "accessories" terminals.

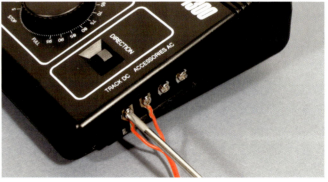

4. Tighten the screws that secure the wires to the power pack.

Running the train

With the track assembled and the feeder wires in place, you're ready to set up the train. With just a few more steps, you'll be running your new set.

   With everything connected, place the locomotive on the rails. Use care to make sure that all the wheels are on the track correctly; this can be a little tricky for newcomers. If one or two wheels are off the track, the locomotive may run, but it will tend to stall or derail.

Use caution with electrical devices

Always observe all electrical precautions included with your power pack. Never plug in a unit with a frayed or damaged cord. Do not unplug the unit by pulling on the cord. Instead, grab the plug assembly and pull straight out from the wall to remove it from the socket. Remember, household electrical current is strong enough to injure or kill, so always use care when you plug in an electrical device.

Rerailers make it easier to place locomotives and cars on the track. These handy devices allow you to roll cars and locomotives onto the rails. Rerailers are often built into terminal track sections, as is the case with the Bachmann E-Z Track section shown here. See your local hobby dealer for a rerailer that is compatible with your brand of track.

1. Plug the power pack into any standard household outlet. Be sure the power pack throttle is set to zero and the unit is switched off if it is equipped with an On/Off switch.

2. Turn on the power pack after you put the locomotive on the rails. Be sure the throttle control is set to zero before flipping the switch. If the model is equipped with an On/Off switch, move the switch to the on position. If it isn't, the power pack will turn on when you plug it into a wall outlet.

3. To run the train, move the speed control throttle from zero to about 50 percent. As you move the throttle, the train starts to move. The more you turn the throttle, the faster the train runs. Conversely, turning the throttle back down to zero cuts power to the track and stops the train.

4. Use the direction switch to control the forward and reverse movement. Flip the switch to the other position to reverse the direction of the train. It's a good idea to stop the train completely before moving the direction switch. Moving this switch while the train is in motion can damage the locomotive or cause the train to derail.

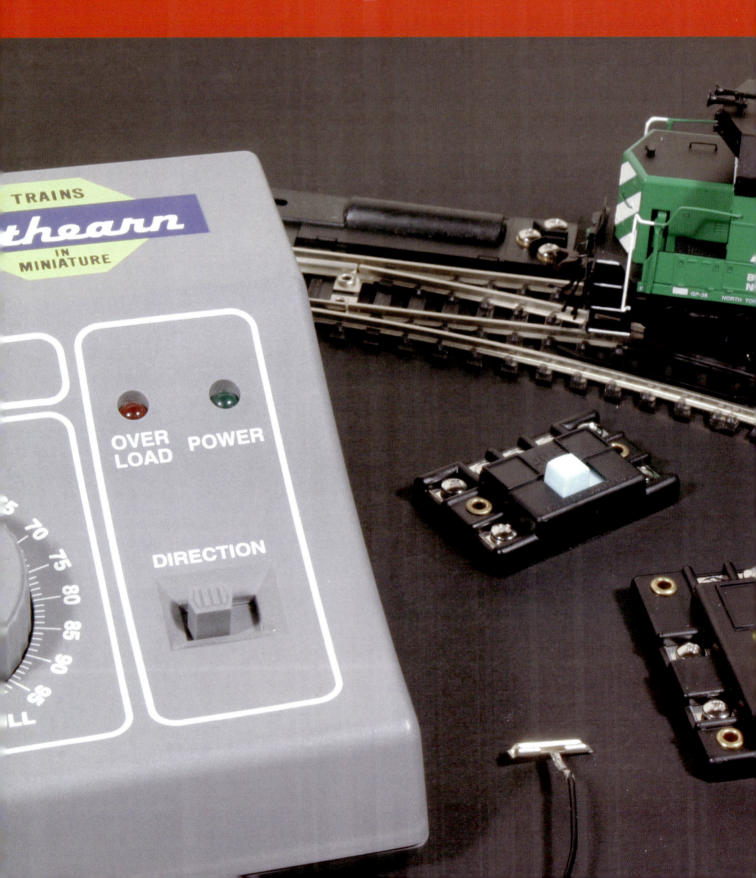

wiring

As you become more interested in the hobby of model railroading, it's inevitable that you will have the urge to expand your layout past the basic oval of track into something that is more enjoyable to operate. When you reach this point, your model railroad's operating potential increases considerably.

Add a few turnouts and spurs, a passing siding, or a second loop of track, and suddenly you've got a layout that has more variety and is more fun to operate. Instead of simply running your locomotive in a circle, you can set out and pick up cars from sidings or operate different locomotives while others rest quietly on a spur track.

However, track configurations that allow this next level of operation sometimes require special wiring in order for the trains to operate properly. Let's take a look at a few of the possibilities you have when expanding your layout and the wiring techniques you can use to make things work properly.

Wiring turnouts

Understanding the basic components of a turnout helps clarify wiring techniques. Turnouts allow a train to travel from one track to another. Called switches on real railroads, turnouts allow you to add spur, yard, and passing tracks to a layout by taking one track and branching it into two.

The main route is called the through route, while the other is called the diverging route. The point rails control the route the train takes through the turnout. The points slide back and forth to rest against the stock rails of the turnout. As the tracks diverge, one rail on each route crosses the other. This occurs at the turnout frog. Guard rails help keep the wheels in check as they move through the frog.

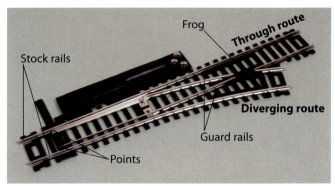

Types of turnouts

Model railroad turnouts come in two basic types – insulated and power-routing. Insulated turnouts (sometimes called standard turnouts) are more common than power-routing (or selective) types, and you may find them easier to install and use. Power-routing turnouts offer a few advantages, but they often require additional wiring to use these features.

You can mix and match turnout types on a layout. You may want to start with insulated turnouts but don't be afraid to mix in a few power-routing turnouts where the added benefits make it worthwhile.

Insulated turnouts route power to both tracks at all times, regardless of the position of the turnout points. Trains on either track leading from a turnout will run any time you operate the throttle on your power pack. The position of the points has no bearing on the way electricity routes through the turnout.

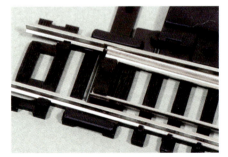
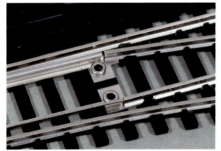

Several characteristics make insulated turnouts easy to identify. The points have no electrical contacts where they meet the stock rails. The frog on these turnouts is typically made of plastic in order to insulate the location where the rails cross and, therefore, does not supply power to locomotive wheels. Hidden electrical contacts molded into the tie sections route power to the two track routes.

Insulated turnouts do not require any special wiring for proper operation. Simply insert them in your layout track plan. Since both tracks are powered at all times, trains will run on either route whenever you apply power to the track.

Power-routing turnouts use contacts and a powered frog to route power to only the route selected by the points. Available for N and HO scales, these turnouts are more versatile, but they require more work to wire properly. There are two big benefits in using power-routing turnouts. Since the frog is metal, it transmits electricity to the locomotive wheels as the train moves through the turnout. This makes your locomotive less sensitive to dirty track. Also, you can use the selective power-routing feature to electrically isolate dead-end sidings and spurs by simply throwing the turnout for the main track.

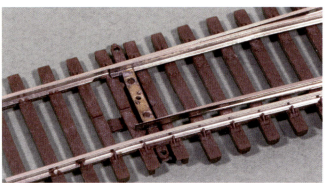

Power-routing turnouts, like this Micro-Engineering model, are easy to identify by examining the turnout frog and the points. These turnouts have a metal frog connected to the adjoining rails. They also typically use copper electrical contacts where the points meet the stock rails. If you are unsure of which turnout you need, ask the staff at your local hobby shop for assistance.

Insulated turnout manufacturers

Manufacturer	HO scale	N scale	O scale	G scale
Atlas	Snap-Switches, Custom Line, Mark III turnouts	Snap-Switches, Custom Line	All turnouts	n/a
Bachmann	E-Z Track turnouts	All turnouts	n/a	n/a
Kato	Some turnouts, optional	Some turnouts, optional	n/a	n/a
LGB	n/a	n/a	n/a	All turnouts
Life-Like	All turnouts	n/a	n/a	n/a
Model Power	All turnouts	n/a	n/a	n/a
Peco	InsulFrog turnouts	InsulFrog turnouts	n/a	n/a
REA	n/a	n/a	n/a	All turnouts
Roco	All turnouts	n/a	n/a	n/a

How power-routing turnouts work

As noted in chapter 1, each rail of your track carries one side of the electrical circuit for your train. Power-routing turnouts control the polarity of the rails that diverge from the turnout. When you set the points to a route, the electrical contacts on the points route electricity through the frog to the appropriate route. As shown, the frog also routes the same polarity to both rails on the nonselected route. This causes an open circuit, and trains on this track don't run. Because of the design, you must feed electrical power to power-routing turnouts from the point end. If you supply power to the frog end of the turnout, the power-routing feature of the turnout won't work, and you'll wind up with a short circuit. This means that when you use a collection of turnouts on your layout, you must use gaps or insulated rail joiners to ensure that you power the turnouts from the point end.

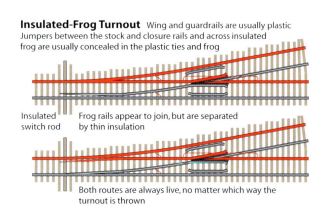

Insulated-Frog Turnout Wing and guardrails are usually plastic Jumpers between the stock and closure rails and across insulated frog are usually concealed in the plastic ties and frog

Insulated switch rod

Frog rails appear to join, but are separated by thin insulation

Both routes are always live, no matter which way the turnout is thrown

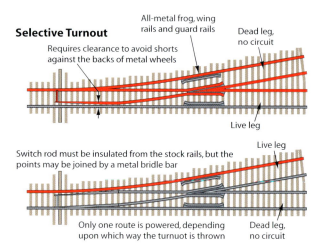

Selective Turnout

All-metal frog, wing rails and guard rails

Requires clearance to avoid shorts against the backs of metal wheels

Dead leg, no circuit

Live leg

Switch rod must be insulated from the stock rails, but the points may be joined by a metal bridle bar

Live leg

Only one route is powered, depending upon which way the turnuot is thrown

Dead leg, no circuit

Power-routing turnout manufacturers		
Manufacturer	**HO scale**	**N scale**
Micro-Engineering	All turnouts	All turnouts
Peco	ElectroFrog turnouts	ElectroFrog turnouts
Shinohara	All turnouts	All turnouts
Walthers	All turnouts	n/a

Wiring isolated track sections

Electrically isolating sections of your layout allows you to park locomotives while you run other trains on your layout. An electrical switch lets you control power to the track, so the parked locomotive runs only when you want it to, while trains on the rest of the layout operate normally.

You have to interrupt only one side of the electrical circuit to prevent a train from running on a track section, usually by disconnecting one rail. If you plan on having more than one isolated track section on your layout, it is a good idea to always use the same rail when placing the insulated rail joiners.

Pick either the inside or outside rail and designate it with a name or color. For example, call it the gap rail. Designate the other rail with a different name or color, such as the common rail. Use the gap rail to create your isolated track sections on all parts of your layout. This consistency helps when troubleshooting, and it makes conversion to multitrain block control (described in chapter 5) much easier.

You can use the same technique shown for passing tracks as well as dead-end spurs. Insert one insulated joiner in the gap rail at each end of the passing track and then install a feeder wire and electrical switch. While the example shown is a simple spur, this technique works just as well for entire yards or switching sections.

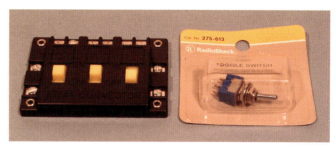

A connector, such as those from Atlas, is an easy-to-use product for controlling a spur track. The connector is a collection of single-pole, single-throw (SPST) toggle switches that allows you to turn track sections, lights, or other accessories on or off. Screw terminals make wire connections quick and easy. One connector is equivalent to three SPST mini toggle switches, shown at right. You can substitute an SPST toggle switch for a connector if it better suits your control panel's design. SPST switches, however, require solder connections.

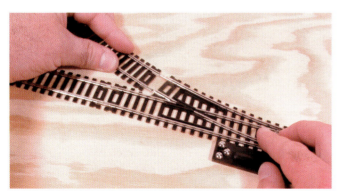

1. To wire a single spur, begin by separating the spur track where it leaves the turnout at the diverging route end and remove the rail joiner from the gap rail.

2. Place an insulated rail joiner in the gap rail. Slide the joiner on all the way so that the plastic pin rests against the end of the rail.

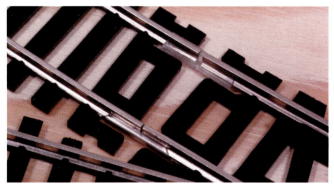

3. Reconnect the track section, guiding the rail into the insulated rail joiner. Make sure the track joint is square and properly aligned.

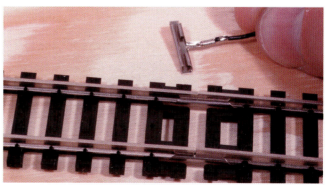

4. Use a rail joiner feeder to supply power to the spur track. These joiners replace the standard rail joiners in your track. You can also use one screw on a terminal track section, if you wish.

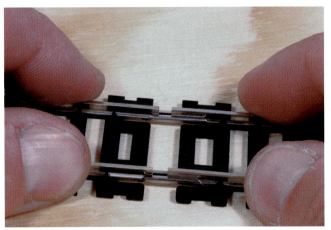

5. Remove the track sections where you decide to place the feeder rail joiner. Remove the rail joiner from the gap rail – the same rail in which you inserted the insulated rail joiner at the turnout.

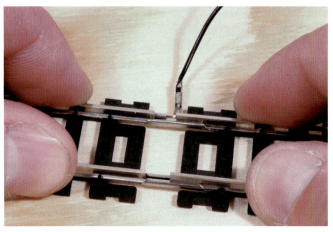

6. Insert the feeder joiner in the track joint and reconnect the track sections.

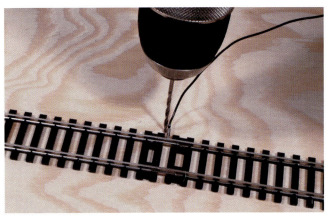

7. With the feeder wire joiners, it's easy to hide the wire and route it underneath the layout to the control switch. Drill a hole next to the feeder wire joiner.

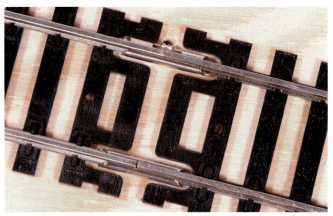

8. Bend the stem of the rail joiner feeder down 90 degrees so that it fits into the hole. Thread the wire down through the hole and then insert the feeder joiner stem into the hole. Once it is installed, the feeder is barely visible (top rail in image).

9. Use the wood screws supplied with the connector to mount it to your control panel surface near your power pack.

10. Connect the rail joiner feeder wire to the right-hand screw terminal on the first switch on the controller. If necessary, solder or splice additional wire to the rail joiner feeder wire to reach your power pack location.

11. Connect a length of wire to the lower screw on the left end of the connector. Drill a hole to route the wire underneath your layout.

12. Connect the other end of this feeder wire to the terminal on your power pack. You must connect this wire to the same terminal that powers the gap rail (the rail with the insulated rail joiner). Trace the wire connections to ensure that you select the proper terminal. With the wires connected, your spur is operational. Set the switch to On to operate a train on the spur track. Set it to Off when you want to park a locomotive or train on this track.

Troubleshooting tips

When trains stop running, it's usually due to a short circuit or an open circuit. Short circuits occur when something, such as a piece of metal across the rails, connects the two sides of the electrical circuit. An open circuit occurs when a wire connection comes loose and prevents voltage from reaching one rail of the track.

Electrical short circuits usually appear as an overload on your power pack. Most units, even inexpensive ones, have an overload indicator of some sort. When this light goes on, it means you have a short circuit condition somewhere in your track circuit. If this occurs, you need to turn the power pack off and search for the cause of the short circuit.

You fix a short circuit by locating and removing whatever is connecting both wires or rails. Check the track for foreign objects such as screws, rail joiners, or detail parts from your rolling stock. If this turns up nothing, inspect the wiring underneath the table. In rare cases, track components can cause short circuits; the only way to identify these defective components is to replace them one by one until you locate the offending part. Always check for obvious causes first when dealing with a short circuit, as it is typically something simple.

Wiring reverse loops

Reverse loops allow a train to traverse a loop of track and re-enter the main line traveling in the opposite direction. As your track plan becomes more complex, you may want to add a reverse loop section to your layout.

Reverse loops present some unique wiring challenges. Remember, you must switch the polarity of the track power in order to make the train reverse direction. But with reverse loops, the train switches direction on its own simply by traveling over the track. If you connect your track to form a reverse loop without adding any insulated rail joiners, you have an instant problem – the positive rail meets the negative rail in the loop, causing a short circuit.

For seamless operation through reverse loops without stopping your train, you must create a separate electrical reversing section controlled by a separate direction switch. You use insulated rail joiners to isolate the reversing section and track feeders to supply power. A dedicated directional switch controls the reversing section. Let's look at the techniques for wiring a basic reverse loop.

Reverse loops can take on many shapes. While many are obvious, others are not. For example, reverse loops are sometimes concealed inside an assortment of other track sections, or the track sections are arranged in such a way that the loop is not obvious to the observer. If in doubt, follow this simple rule – if the train can reverse direction by traversing a particular section of track, you have a reverse loop and should follow the following special wiring guidelines.

Reverse loops in disguise

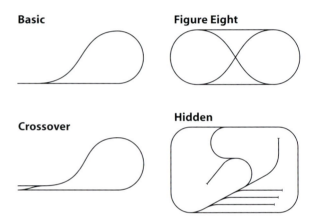

Basic

Figure Eight

Crossover

Hidden

The Atlas Twin is a collection of double-pole, double-throw (DPDT) switches that you can use for wiring reversing sections and turntables. Screw terminals make wire connection quick and easy. One Twin is equivalent to two DPDT mini toggle switches. You can substitute two DPDT switches for a Twin if the toggle switches better fit your control panel design.

1. Remove the track sections where they leave the reverse loop turnout.

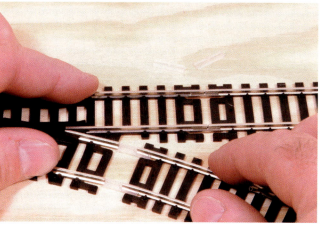

2. Install an insulated rail joiner on both rails of each track. Slide the joiners on all the way so that the plastic pin rests against the end of the rail.

3. Reconnect the track sections to the turnout. Carefully guide the rails into the insulated rail joiners. Make sure the track connections are secure and properly aligned.

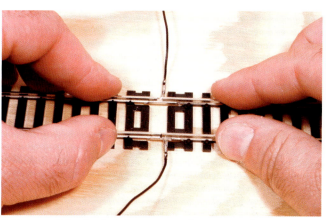

4. Use two Atlas feeder joiners to supply power to the reversing section, one in each rail. You can place the two feeder joiners anywhere between the insulated rail joiners. If you want, you can conceal the feeder stems by drilling a hole and bending the stems down 90 degrees, so they fit into the holes.

5. Mount the Atlas Twin on the control panel surface near your power pack using the wood screws supplied with the component. Drill holes to accommodate the wires.

6. If you wired one or more spur tracks through the Atlas Connector, disconnect the feeder wire for the connector from the terminal screw on your power pack.

7. Connect feeder wires from your power pack track terminals to the input terminals on the Atlas Twin.

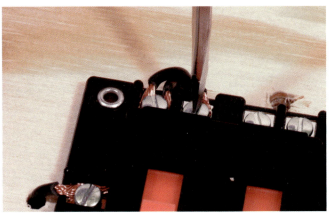

8. Connect the feeder wires from the layout to the left set of terminals on top of the Twin. The left switch controls the direction for the main layout section. If you wired the connector as described, attach the connector's feeder wire to the screw terminal that corresponds to the gap rail on the main section of the layout.

9. Connect the feeder wires from the reversing section to the right set of terminals on the Twin. If necessary, solder or splice additional wire to the feeder wires to reach your power pack location. The right switch controls the direction for the reversing loop section.

10. With the wires connected, your reversing loop is ready to run. Use the directional switches on the Twin to control the direction of your train on the main line and reversing loop sections. You can wire additional reversing loops (or wye tracks) using additional Twins connected to the right side terminals on the first Twin with the supplied connectors.

Operating reversing loops

Operating the reverse loop is easy. Set both Twin switches to the same position to align the main layout polarity with the polarity for the reversing section. After a train enters the reversing section, throw the mainline directional (left) switch on the Twin. Leave the reversing section (right) switch in its original position. This reverses the polarity on the main layout. As the train leaves the reversing section and reenters the main section, the rail polarities match, and the train runs without interruption.

Wye tracks

A wye is a triangular-shaped track arrangement used for turning locomotives. Wye tracks allow a train to do the equivalent of a three-point turn, reversing direction as it moves through the track sections. Since the locomotive reverses direction, wye tracks need the same wiring as return loops.

Reversing Section

To Twin

Feeders

Wiring a wye. You wire a wye track just as you do a return loop. Select a leg of the wye to be the reversing section. Isolate both rails of this section with insulated rail joiners. Attach feeders to the isolated section, then connect the feeder wires to one set of switch terminals on an Atlas Twin. Connect the other Twin terminals to the main layout. Finally, connect the power pack to the power inputs on the Atlas Twin. Use the switch on the Atlas Twin to control the direction on the reversing section of the wye track.

Turntable tracks

Turntables are another popular track component modelers can add to their layouts. You can use an Atlas Twin to wire the turntable bridge for independent reversing of this track section. This allows you to operate locomotives off the turntable bridge, no matter which direction they are facing.

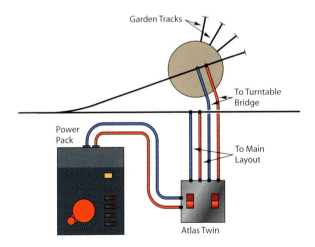

Garden Tracks

To Turntable Bridge

Power Pack

To Main Layout

Atlas Twin

Wiring a turntable. Wire the turntable bridge track in the same way as a reversing loop and wye tracks. You can also use a connector to wire on/off switches for the turntable garden tracks. This allows you to park locomotives on these tracks while you operate the rest of the layout.

Basic block wiring

CHAPTER 5

A layout with one train can definitely be enjoyable. But the desire to operate more than one train at a time eventually enters the minds of most model railroaders. Maybe you want to share the fun of operating your layout with a friend or family member. Or maybe you simply want to get more operational variety by running two independently controlled trains on one layout.

The idea of running two trains under independent control on the same layout may sound complicated, but it's actually easy to do. In chapter 4, we looked at wiring isolated track sections so you can park a locomotive while running another train. In this chapter, we'll implement a technique that allows you to run multiple trains under independent control anywhere on a layout. This technique is called block wiring.

Block wiring

With block wiring, you divide your layout into electrical sections, or blocks, and wire each of them through a control switch, so you determine which control cab operates that block. This allows you to run multiple trains with independent control so long as both trains don't enter the same electrical block simultaneously.

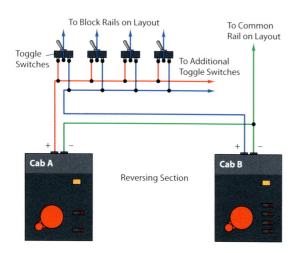

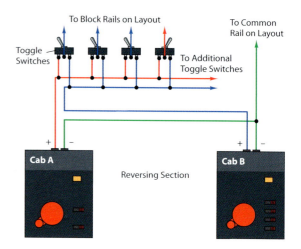

Common-rail wiring. This technique simplifies the block wiring scheme and allows you to implement block wiring using less wire. With common-rail wiring, you divide one rail, called the block rail, into electrical blocks. To install this wiring, you connect feeder wires to the block rail in each block and then connect the feeders to toggle switches. The toggle switches connect to one terminal on each of two power packs on your layout (A and B in the example). You wire the other rail, called the common rail, directly to the same terminal on each power pack.

How it works. When set to either position, the toggle switches route power from either power pack A or power pack B to the track block. If a toggle switch is set to A, the circuit for power pack A is closed in that block, and power pack A can run a train. At the same time, any blocks set to B receive power from power pack B. The common rail carries one side of the circuit for each power pack, allowing two trains to operate independently as long as they are in different blocks.

Creating track blocks

To create a track block, you must electrically isolate the block rail in that block from the block rails in adjoining blocks. There are several ways to create track blocks. The easiest method is to use insulated rail joiners. You can also cut the rail in the appropriate place using a razor saw or a handheld motor tool with a cutoff disk.

The first step in installing block wiring is to identify the appropriate location for your track blocks. There really are no solid rules on block location. When deciding where to place blocks, you must think about how you plan to operate the layout. For example, do you want to be able to park locomotives on sidings or on passing tracks, or do you want to be able to run multiple trains on the same loop of track?

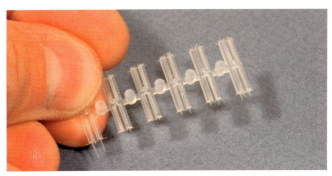

You can use insulated rail joiners to create your track blocks. Insert the rail joiners in the appropriate locations (as described in chapter 3) and then reassemble your track sections. By using the insulated rail joiners, you can always go back later and adjust block boundaries by moving the joiners. This also gives you the chance to test your block design to be sure it works as you intended.

Locating your blocks

You want to locate your block boundaries in logical locations that allow you to operate your layout the way you want. Since you need to keep each train in a separate block, you need to consider the block boundary locations based on your track plan's configuration. Typical block boundary locations might include the end of passing tracks, yard segments, switching areas, or crossovers between two main tracks. One option for block boundary placement on a simple 4 x 8 layout is shown.

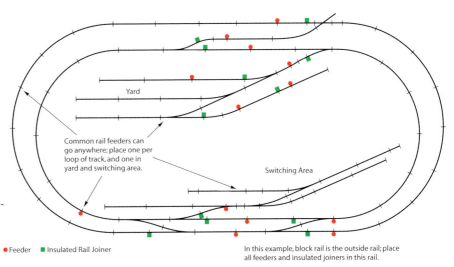

Yard

Common rail feeders can go anywhere; place one per loop of track, and one in yard and switching area.

Switching Area

● Feeder ■ Insulated Rail Joiner

In this example, block rail is the outside rail; place all feeders and insulated joiners in this rail.

If you don't want to remove your track sections to install insulated rail joiners, or if you are sure about the location of your block boundaries, you can cut gaps in your rails to create electrical blocks. A razor saw or motor tool with a cutoff wheel makes quick work of cutting rail. Always wear safety goggles when using the cutoff wheel to prevent injury from flying debris or a broken cutoff wheel.

Connecting feeders

With the blocks in place, it's time to hook up new feeder wires to your track sections. Again, there are several ways to connect feeders to your rails.

One way is to insert feeder rail joiners (a minimum of one in each block section). Rail joiner feeders work well if you are using sectional track or if you can easily remove track sections that you've already installed.

Those comfortable with their soldering skills can solder feeder wires directly to the rails. This option works well if you're using flextrack on your layout or if you have previously ballasted your track, which makes it difficult to remove without damage.

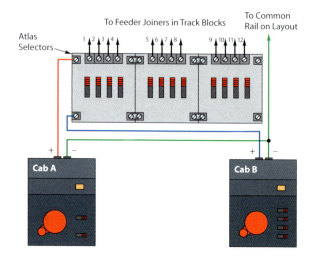

Wiring the blocks to the selectors. This is a simple and straight-forward process. First, connect power packs to the terminals on the left side of the selectors and then connect the track blocks to the terminals on top of the selectors.

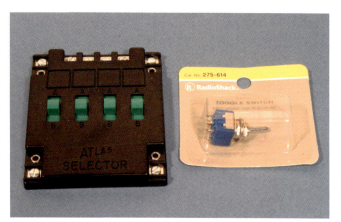

To wire track blocks, you can use Atlas Selector components. An Atlas Selector is the equivalent of four single-pole, double-throw (SPDT), center off toggle switches in one housing. You can use SPDT toggle switches in place of the selector if they are better suited to your control panel design, but you will need to solder wires to the switch contacts.

Use the same techniques described in chapter 4 to install feeder wire joiners in the block rails in each track block. Use terminal rail joiners or solder feeder wires directly to the block rails. The soldering method comes in handy for track sections that you don't want to remove or contain ballast or solder joints between track sections.

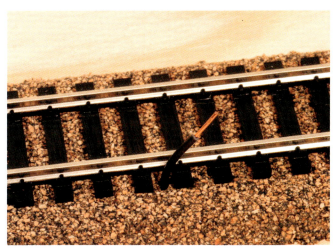

1. To start, drill a hole alongside the rail for the feeder wire. Route the feeder wire through the hole from underneath the layout. Strip the insulation from the wire, then bend the conductor 90 degrees so that it lies next to the rail. Apply some flux to the wire and rail, then solder the wire to the side of the rail (described in chapter 2). Use a needlenose pliers to hold the wire in place until the solder cools.

2. You have to add a second power pack in order to control two trains on your layout. Any power pack will work as long as it is compatible with the scale you are using. This example shows an MRC Tech 4 200 as our second throttle.

3. Mount the Atlas Selectors directly onto a flat control panel surface, using the small wood screws provided. Drill holes in the control panel to allow the feeder wires to run underneath the control panel surface. The selectors are designed to gang together end to end, eliminating the need to run feeders to each component. Assemble enough selectors to control all the blocks.

4. Connect one terminal of power pack A to the top terminal on the left side of the selector.

5. Connect one terminal of power pack B to the lower terminal on the left side of the connector.

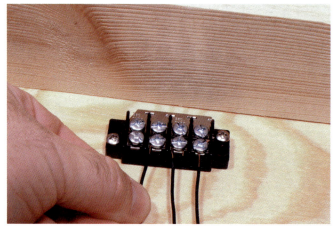

6. Connect the remaining terminals from each power pack together. You can use a terminal strip underneath the control panel area to join the common wires together, or you can solder the connections. This example shows a four-position terminal strip with bus bar. Connect these wires to the common rail on the layout in at least one location.

7. After connecting feeder wires to each block rail, run these wires to the control panel and attach them to the selector to connect each block. To operate the blocks, set the switch to either the Up or Down position in order to connect one of the power packs to that block. You can turn a block off altogether by placing the switch in the center position.

Operating a layout with block control

Chapter 4 described how to wire reverse loops and wye tracks on layouts that use a single power pack, or cab. Wiring these track configurations becomes more complicated when you install common-rail block wiring for multiple cabs.

Operating a layout with block control takes a little practice, but it's easy once you get the hang of it. To start, select a route for your train, identifying the blocks it must travel over. Next, move the switches for the blocks on the train's route to the cab you want to use (A or B). Use the corresponding cab to run the train. Then, do the same for the second train, setting the block controls accordingly. You can switch the block controls at any time, even while a train is running; this allows you to assign blocks to a train as it runs around your layout. If you installed any Atlas controllers, use the directional switches on the controller to set the direction of the trains, not the directional switches on your power packs.

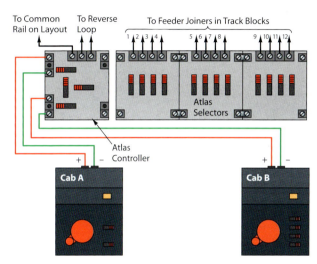

1. The controller is designed to mount ahead of the selectors. Place one controller on your control panel for each reverse loop or wye on your layout. Connect enough selectors to the controller to support all the blocks on your layout.

2. Connect both track terminals on each of your power packs to the controller. Once it's installed, the controller handles all directional control for the layout – you do not use the directional switches on the power packs.

3. Connect the feeders from the reversing section to the two right terminals on top of the controller. The controller also handles the common-rail feed; you must connect a wire from the common rail to the C terminal on top of the controller. To operate the reverse loop, you use the gray directional switch. To change direction on either cab, you use the two red directional switches. The green switch selects the cab that controls the reverse loop.

with DCC

The train control systems discussed until now use the same principle to control the train: the throttle varies the voltage to the rails, making the motor change rotational speed, which, in turn, alters speed of the locomotive. Put another way – if there is voltage on the track, the train runs.

But what if you could control the train from inside the locomotive itself? What if you didn't have to go through all the effort to connect block control wiring so you can run multiple trains? What if you had the flexibility to run your train anywhere on the layout without worrying about block and power controls?

Digital Command Control systems, or DCC for short, allow you to do just this. They work on any scale, are relatively simple to install, and allow more operational flexibility than conventional block control. And many more locomotives are coming direct from the factory ready to operate on DCC systems.

DCC operation and components

In basic form, DCC operation is straightforward:

- The throttle sends a control signal to the command station.
- The command station arranges the control signal according to the DCC protocol and sends it to the booster.
- The booster unit amplifies the signal and feeds it to the track.
- The track carries the digital signal through the rails to the locomotive.
- The decoder in the locomotive reads the control signal message and executes the command.

All control of the locomotive occurs in the decoder. If a digital message is addressed to a locomotive's decoder, the decoder processes the message and sets the motor voltage accordingly.

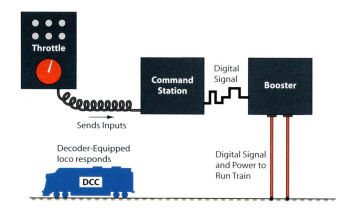

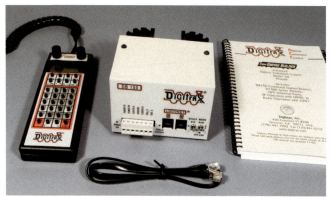

DCC starter systems are available from several manufacturers. They vary in price, features, and appearance, but they all need a few basic components: a throttle, a command station, a booster unit, and a digital decoder or decoder-equipped locomotive.

DCC throttles come in different shapes and configurations, but they all serve the same purpose – they control the speed and direction of your train as it operates. Some throttles use knobs for speed control, such as the Digitrax unit shown here, and some use buttons. Many systems also allow you to control special effects such as headlights and warning lights on locomotives that are equipped with them.

Hand-held throttles typically rely upon a cable and plug to connect to the command station. Most systems allow you to add multiple plugs at different locations around your layout. The Lenz system components, shown here, use a 5-pin DIN connector for connecting the throttle. Other systems, like those from Digitrax

and NCE, use standard 6-conductor telephone cable and RJ-25 connectors to add additional throttle connection points. And for most systems, you can purchase throttles that communicate via radio signals or infrared light, eliminating the need for a cable altogether.

Command station and booster units

The command station is the brain of a DCC system. The command station processes control inputs from the throttle. When the operator increases the train speed, the command station receives the signal from the throttle and formats a digital message for the locomotive decoder. It passes this signal on to the booster unit.

Booster units provide power to the track. They take the control signal from the command station, combine it with power, and route it to the rails. Some booster units offer additional features such as voltage regulation and overload protection. Many systems package the command station and booster unit in the same housing.

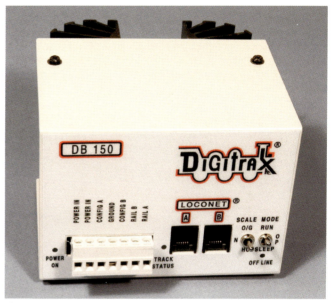

The Digitrax DB-150 unit contains the command and booster unit. It also features front-panel connections which make installation straightforward. Other systems also combine the components in one housing, while some require the purchase of a separate command station and booster unit.

Safety first!

Use extreme care when wiring 110-volt electrical connections. Improperly wired 110-volt household circuits pose a risk of fire and can injure or kill. If you have doubts about your abilities to wire these connections safely and properly, consult a professional electrician or buy a prewired power supply.

Power supply

Many DCC systems do not include a power supply, so you'll have to buy a transformer capable of supplying the correct voltage and current to operate the layout.

You have several options, and the simplest one is to use a traditional power pack to supply current to the booster unit. For most small layouts, this option works fine. For medium to large layouts, or those that run multiple trains, you should purchase a transformer that is compatible with your DCC system.

The specific voltage and current output of the transformer varies depending upon the DCC system you are using. For example, Digitrax recommends a transformer with an output of 12 to 20 volts AC or 12 to 28 volts DC, at a maximum of 5 amps, for its systems. Be sure to buy a unit that supplies the correct voltage as specified by the DCC manufacturer.

This transformer supplies 13.8 volts DC and a current output of 3 amps. It also includes an On/Off switch and a fuse and comes prewired for 110-volt operation. Just plug it in, connect the output wires, and you are ready to go.

Decoders

Locomotive decoders come in many shapes and sizes. Most decoders built today are designed to be compatible with the National Model Railroad Association (NMRA) Standards and Recommended Practices. Generally speaking, DCC-compatible decoders work with any DCC-compatible system. In other words, if you purchase a Digitrax DCC starter system, you can use locomotive decoders from Lenz, NCE, MRC, or others.

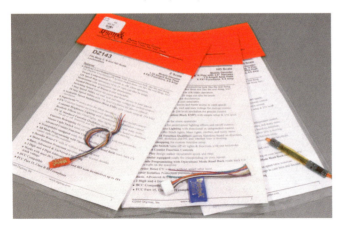

Accessory decoders, such as the Digitrax unit shown here, allow you to control switch machines and other lighted or motorized accessories using your DCC system. Instead of wiring each of these accessories separately, you can control them with the same digital signals through the track that you use to control the trains.

Connecting DCC systems

At a basic level, wiring a DCC system on your layout is generally a much easier task than connecting block wiring. In theory, you can connect the two track output wires to the rails and start running trains.

At a practical level, however, there are a few more considerations you must take into account, regardless of your layout size. These decisions are easiest to make before you install your system because changing things later can render some of your equipment obsolete or ineffective.

In theory, you can leave your entire layout as one large electrical block, connect the wires from the booster unit, and start running trains. In fact, this approach works just fine on small layouts.

However, if you have a larger layout with lots of turnouts or other complicated track configurations, there are benefits to dividing your layout into electrical blocks. For instance, when troubleshooting, it is advantageous to isolate portions of the layout to help identify problems. You can also park locomotives on storage sections of track and completely isolate them electrically, preventing accidental operation.

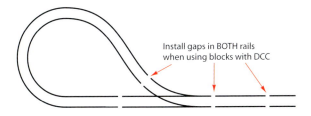

Install gaps in BOTH rails when using blocks with DCC

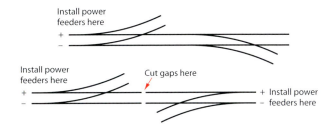

Install power feeders here

Install power feeders here

Cut gaps here

Install power feeders here

Block a layout. If you choose to block your layout, use the techniques described in chapter 5 to gap the rails at the block boundaries. Use insulated rail joiners or cut gaps in the track at the desired location. However, with DCC, you must install gaps in both rails at all locations to completely isolate the blocks and prevent short circuits.

Wire a power-routing turnout. As explained in chapter 4, power-routing turnouts require special wiring, and this is true even with DCC systems. You must supply power to these turnouts from the point end, and you must cut gaps into power-routing turnouts so they operate properly.

Wiring example – Digitrax Empire Builder system

The Digitrax Empire Builder DCC system is designed with beginners in mind. It is a full-featured DCC system that allows you to add additional components as your layout grows. While the techniques shown are specific to the Digitrax connections, other DCC systems are similar in design and comparably easy to connect to your layout.

However, before installing any DCC system, be sure to thoroughly read the instructions. Installation requirements and techniques differ slightly from system to system, so you should use the steps shown here only as a guide.

Let's look at the steps in connecting a Digitrax Empire Builder system.

1. Connect the feeder wires to your power supply. Position the power supply near where you intend to mount the DCC command unit and near a wall outlet. Leave the power off for now.

2. Connect the leads from the power supply to the power inputs on the screw terminals on the front of the DB150. Tighten the screw connectors, so they hold the wire securely.

3. Connect feeder wires to the rail outputs on the front of the DB150. Use heavy-gauge wire; the wire shown here is 16 gauge. Run the rail feeder wires under the layout to connect with your track feeders.

4. Use a terminal strip under the layout to distribute power to the track blocks as necessary. If you previously wired your layout for block control, you can connect all the blocks under the layout using a terminal strip and bus bar, as shown here. If you haven't created blocks on your layout, you can simply connect the track output from the DCC booster directly to the rails.

5. With your track connections complete, plug in the throttle to one of the LocoNet jacks. Remember, you can add additional LocoNet throttle jacks using the Digitrax UP-5 Universal Panel and 6-conductor telephone cable.

6. Your Empire Builder system is ready to go. Turn on the power supply and then operate the throttle according to the instructions. Be sure to read the Digitrax instructions thoroughly so you understand the features and functions available.

Isolating reverse loops and wyes

With DCC systems, you still must isolate reverse loops and wye tracks as described in chapter 4. Without these gaps, these track configurations still cause short circuits.

However, there's an easy way to wire these sections on DCC layouts – auto-reversing units. These units monitor track polarity in reversing loop or wye track sections. Upon detecting a train, these units automatically flip the polarity of the track section, so the train keeps operating. You don't have to do anything other than run the train.

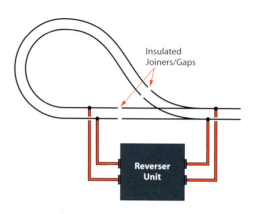

Insulated Joiners/Gaps

Reverser Unit

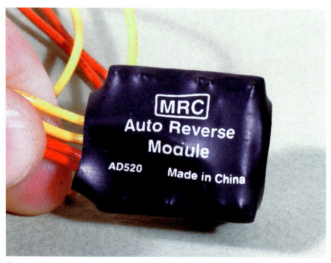

Auto-reversing units manage the track polarity for DCC reversing sections. Most units, like the MRC model shown here, have just two pairs of wires or track inputs. To install an auto-reversing unit, connect one pair of track inputs to the main section of your layout. Connect the other track inputs to the reversing section. Use feeder joiners or soldered feeders to connect the wires to the rails. That's all there is to it – the auto-reversing unit does the rest.

Factory decoders

With the rapid rise in popularity of DCC systems, many manufacturers now offer locomotives with DCC decoders installed direct from the factory. Many of these units also come with sound-equipped decoders that allow you to easily enjoy sound effects with your locomotives.

Often when locomotives ship with factory decoders, they have jumpers installed that allow the unit to operate on traditional DC layouts. On the Atlas GP38, you can access the DCC decoder by popping off the dynamic brake hatch on the locomotive shell. Other units might require you to remove the shell entirely to access the decoder. To remove the jumpers, follow the instructions that come with your locomotive.

The Atlas GP38 shown here includes a factory installed DCC decoder.

Installing locomotive decoders

Installing locomotive decoders often proves to be the most difficult part of DCC installation. However, with the continued miniaturization of electronic equipment, it is becoming much easier to install decoders in crowded locomotive shells.

The following pages show examples of decoder installation in select N and HO scale locomotives. For the most part, the installation techniques shown here can be used in almost any locomotive you want to equip for DCC.

When in doubt, talk to the staff at your local hobby shop about recommendations for a particular locomotive. Some shops even offer a decoder installation service if you decide you don't want to do it yourself.

Installing receivers in some N scale locomotives is a straight-forward process. The Atlas GP40-2 is one of these units since Digitrax makes a decoder specifically designed to drop right in. Installation takes less than 15 minutes and allows you to install a decoder without altering the locomotive frame.

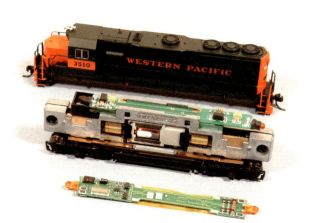

1. To start, remove the locomotive shell. Grab the fuel tank and pull the shell up off the frame. After you remove the shell, you can see the factory circuit board for the locomotive lights.

2. Separate the locomotive frame sections and remove the factory circuit board from the frame. Use care when handling the drive train parts. Insert the decoder into one half of the frame, then mate the other half of the frame back to the mechanism. Use care not to bend or damage the brass motor contacts.

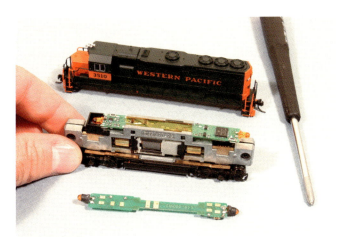

3. Insert the decoder into the frame as shown and then reassemble the frame and trucks. Replace the locomotive shell to complete installation.

Custom N scale installation?

For those N scale locomotives not readily equipped to accept a decoder, you often must make extensive modifications to the locomotive mechanism so a decoder fits. Several manufacturers offer decoders, such as the Digitrax DZ143 and the DN163 (shown below), sized for N scale locomotives. In many cases, even with small decoders, you must modify the locomotive frame so they fit. For this reason, installing decoders in many N scale locomotives is a task best left to experienced modelers. Check with your local hobby shop to see if they offer custom DCC decoder installation.

Decoder wire color codes

Wire color	Function	DCC socket pin
Orange	Right rail motor lead	1
Yellow	Rear headlight	2
Black	Left rail pickup	4
Gray	Left rail motor pickup	5
White	Forward headlight	6
Blue	Front/Rear headlight common	7
Red	Right rail pickup	8
Green	Function 1 output	n/a
Violet	Function 2 output	n/a

Note: Pin 3 on DCC socket not used

Locomotives with NMRA DCC socket

Virtually all new HO locomotives manufactured today feature a standard NMRA decoder socket, making decoder installation easy. To install decoders in these locomotives, you remove the dummy plug from the factory circuit board and plug a decoder into the socket. Manufacturers such as Digitrax, Lenz, and NCE offer decoders that plug into these NMRA sockets.

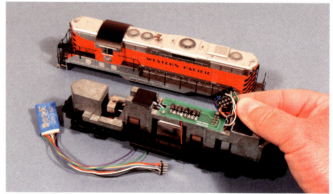

When you're installing decoders, some locomotives require a few extra steps. The Life-Like HO Scale GP7 is one example. It uses the standard socket, but you must remove the factory lighting circuit board before installing the decoder. Take out the board by removing the screws and pulling it from the frame. Plug a decoder into the NMRA socket on the small circuit board, secure the decoder on the frame where the factory board was positioned and then replace the locomotive shell.

Installing a decoder in a Kato HO scale SD38-2

Installing decoders in DCC socket-equipped locomotives is a straightforward process. You can equip a DCC-ready locomotive in just a few minutes using a decoder from a number of manufacturers. Let's look at decoder installation in a Kato HO scale SD38-2.

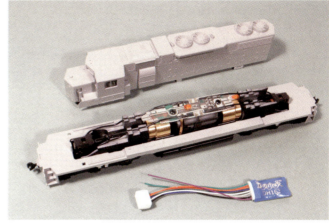

1. Remove the locomotive shell. Locate the socket on the factory circuit board. On most Kato units like the SD38-2 shown here, the socket is located right above the rear portion of the motor.

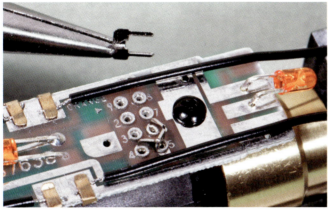

2. Remove the dummy plug or jumpers from the DCC socket. The Kato SD38-2 has two metal 3-pin jumpers that must be removed when installing a DCC decoder in the socket. Use a needlenose pliers to pull the pins out of the socket.

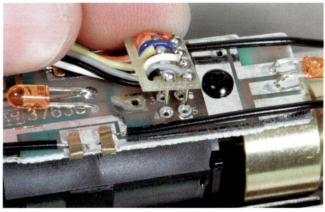

3. Insert the decoder plug into the DCC socket. Orient the plug in the proper direction so the red and black leads connect to the track and the gray and orange leads connect to the motor. The orange lead should connect to pin 1 on the socket, which is typically marked with a small triangle.

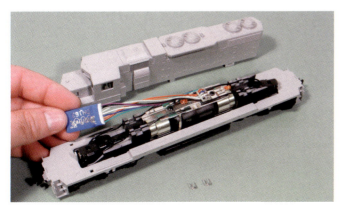

4. After checking the connection – an improper connection can damage the decoder – the unit is ready for reassembly.

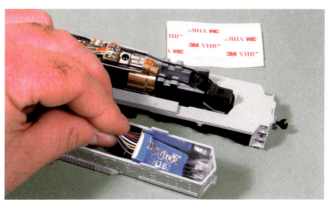

5. Mount the decoder inside the locomotive shell using double-stick tape. After replacing the shell, you are ready to program the decoder and operate the locomotive.

Using a wiring harness

Some popular older locomotives, from manufacturers such as Athearn, may not be equipped with factory decoder plugs. Regardless, receiver installation is easy if you use a wiring harness offered especially for these units. Let's look at decoder installation in an HO scale Athearn C44-9W.

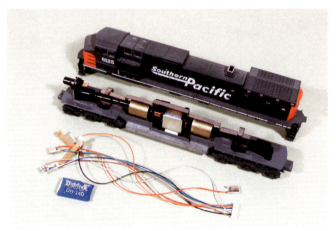

1. Begin a solderless installation on all Athearn locomotives by removing the shell.

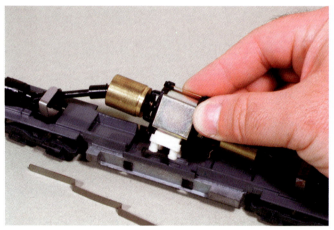

2. Next, snap off the metal contact strip that spans the motor and trucks. Then, lift the motor and flywheel assembly from the frame by pulling it straight up. The drive shaft universals come out with the motor.

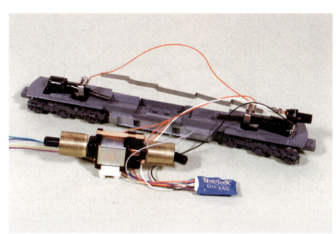

3. With the motor out of the frame, remove the top copper clip from the motor housing. Use care so you do not lose the spring and motor brush. Snap the new Digitrax clip attached to the orange wire in place on the locomotive motor. Repeat this process with the bottom motor clip and then reinstall the motor in the Athearn frame.

4. Attach the Digitrax clips to the truck tabs, headlight, and headlight mount and then secure the decoder inside the locomotive shell. Replace the locomotive shell to complete the installation.

Decoder programming tips

Most decoders come from the manufacturer with a preprogrammed address of 03. In order to control multiple trains on a layout, you must program new decoders with a unique address.

You can select any number of address configurations, but a simple guideline is to use the last two digits of the locomotive number. You can also program many decoders to support operating headlights and accessory lights.

Typically, when programming decoders, you must program them on a programming track isolated from the rest of the layout. If you attempt to program a new decoder with other DCC locomotives on the track, you run the risk of reprogramming all of them. Follow the instructions with your DCC system to connect and use a programming track.

The specific programming tasks differ from system to system. Read the instructions thoroughly before attempting to program a new decoder.

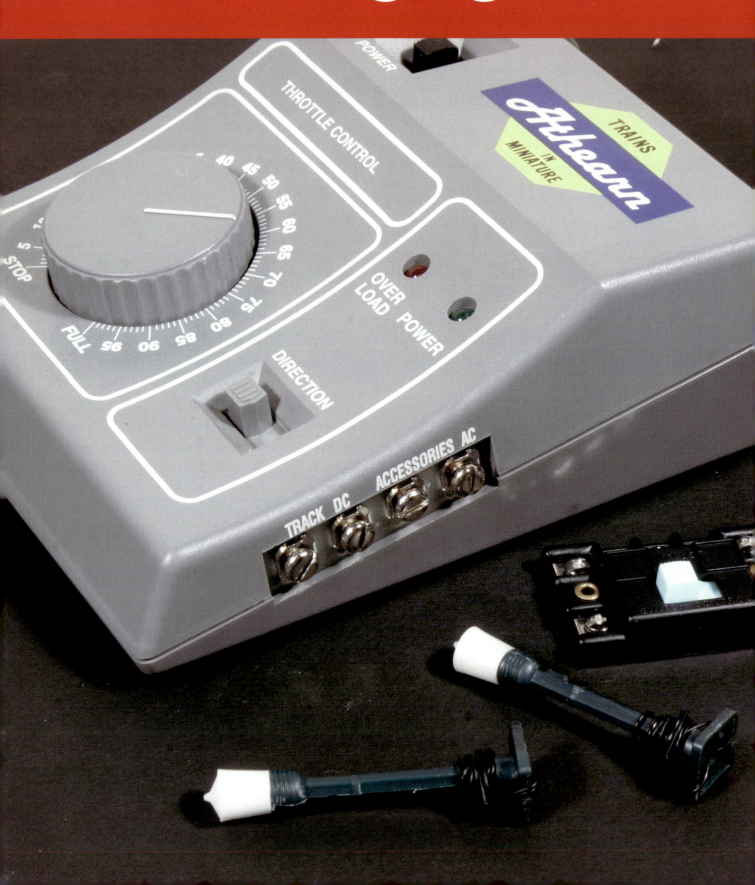

accessories

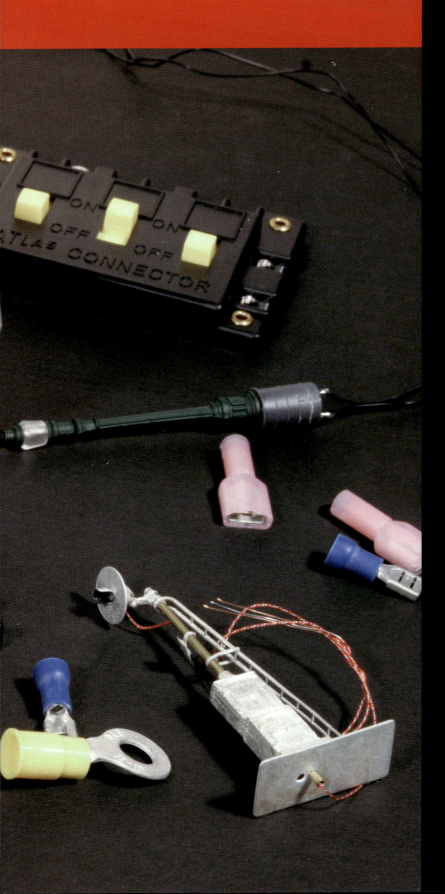

Accessories such as turnout motors, lights, and signals can really bring your layout to life, and they make running trains more fun.

Installing powered accessories is not difficult once you understand the basics of connecting them to the power supply. And you often use the same techniques in wiring accessories that you use in wiring track. By planning ahead in your installations, you can add accessories quickly and easily by connecting them to your existing wiring infrastructure.

Let's look at a few examples of accessory installation, starting with turnout motors.

Wiring solenoid switch motors

Remote control turnouts use solenoid motors that automatically move the points to change the route of the train. Turnouts from companies such as Atlas and Bachmann allow you to change the route of a train from the control panel, no matter where the turnout is located.

Solenoid turnout mechanisms are reliable, and the fact that they're inexpensive makes them popular with beginning and intermediate modelers. Readily available, they're found on virtually any remote control switch that you might buy at your local hobby shop.

Wiring them is easy, so let's look at the steps for connecting solenoid switch motors.

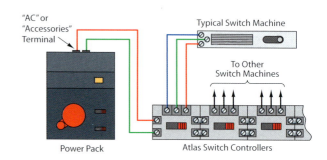

"AC" or "Accessories" Terminal

Typical Switch Machine

To Other Switch Machines

Power Pack

Atlas Switch Controllers

Solenoid mechanisms operate with three wires. One wire serves as the common, while the other two energize one side of the coil mechanism to throw the switch. Installation is easy. First, drill a hole alongside the screw terminals on the turnout mechanism for the wires. Route the wires through the hole. Strip the wire insulation from the leads and connect the wires to the turnout mechanism according to the turnout instructions. Then route the wires to the control switch on the control panel.

It's best to use three-conductor cable to wire switch machines, since it helps keep the installation neat, as shown. You can also use individual wires or three-conductor flat wire. Any wire that's 22-24 gauge or heavier will work.

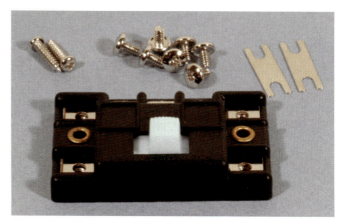

Most solenoid-powered turnouts come with momentary push-button control units that operate the turnout. When you push the button, the solenoid energizes and the turnout throws.

The example shown here is made by Atlas, but other manufacturers use similar controllers. This Atlas control is also available separately and will operate all brands of solenoid-powered turnouts.

1. To start installation, drill a hole alongside the screw terminals on the switch machine motor and then feed the three-conductor cable up through the hole. Next, strip the cable insulation from the wire using a hobby knife, being careful not to nick any insulation on the individual wires, so the inside wires can be connected to the screws. Then strip the insulation from the ends of each individual wire using a wire stripper.

2. Attach the wires to the screw terminals on the switch motor. In the example, the yellow wire is the common, so attach it to the middle screw terminal. Attach the green wire, which corresponds to the straight route through the turnout, to the outside screw terminal. The red wire, corresponding to the diverging route, connects to the inside terminal. After you attach the wires to the terminals, pull the excess wire back down through the hole in your tabletop.

3. Mount the switch control box on your control panel in a location that is easy to access. It should also be near your power supply to minimize the amount of wire you have to run.

4. Drill a hole next to the control box to allow the wire to reach the terminals. Make sure you use a bit that's larger than the wire cable you are using.

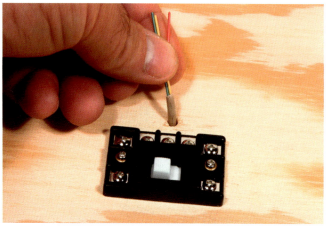

5. Route the wire under your layout and then feed it up through the hole alongside the three screw terminals on the switch control box.

6. Strip the cable insulation from the wire bundle and then strip the insulation from each wire. Attach the wires to the control box terminal screws. In our example, connect the yellow common wire to the middle terminal, the green wire to the left terminal, and the red wire to the right terminal.

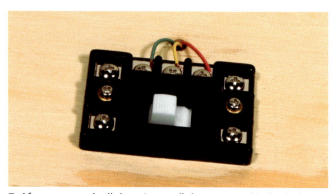

7. After you attach all the wires, pull the excess cable back down through the layout surface. Be careful not to pull the wire loose from the screw terminals.

8. Connect power from the Accessories or AC terminal on your power pack to the two screw terminals on the left side of the switch control box. Turn the power on, and when you push the button, your turnout should throw automatically.

Wiring multiple switches

The Atlas switch machine controls are designed to be ganged on your control panel. Assemble the control switches as shown using the supplied blade connectors, and then mount them on your control panel. Then, connect the power leads from the Accessories/AC terminal on your power pack. Finally, connect the leads from the turnout mechanisms to the screw terminals on each control box.

You can also wire multiple turnouts through one switch where you want two turnouts to always throw together. To install, simply connect the wires from both switches to the same control box terminals.

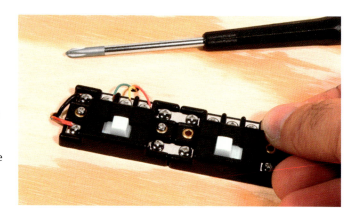

Adding other motors and accessories

Slow-motion turnout motors are designed for use with a variety of different turn-outs. These slow-motion motor drive turnout mechanisms, such as the Tortoise machine shown here, require more complicated wiring than solenoid machines, but they are much quieter and more reliable long-term. In order to wire these motors, you must add a toggle switch to control the turnout direction. To wire these units, follow the instructions that accompany the product.

Turnout motors require some modeling skill to install, but if you want to use certain brands of switches, you might have to consider these motors.

Lighted accessories

Many companies offer a variety of lighted and animated accessories that you can add to your model railroad. Examples include streetlights, railroad signals, crossing gates, structure lights, and other lighting effects. Most lighted items operate on either AC or DC current.

Streetlights are popular accessories for model railroads. Most of these lights are designed to operate at 12 to 18 volts, and they operate on either AC or DC power. Installation of these lights is a straightforward process.

Wiring streetlights

1. Drill a hole in your layout tabletop and feed the streetlight wires down through the hole. Use glue to fix the streetlight in place if necessary; be careful not to get glue on the wires where they travel through the table. If you accidentally glue these wires, it will be extremely difficult to remove the light should you ever need to replace the bulb.

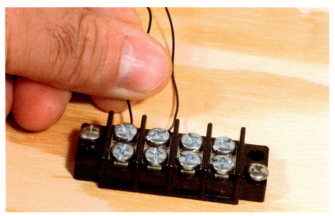

2. Most streetlights have short wire leads, generally less than one foot, and in many cases, that's not enough to reach the power supply. In order to connect these accessories, you may have to add additional wire to connect these lights to your power pack. One way is using a terminal strip to make the wire connections. Attach the wires from the light to one set of terminal screws on the terminal strip. You could also solder the wires together or use mechanical crimp connectors (see chapter 8).

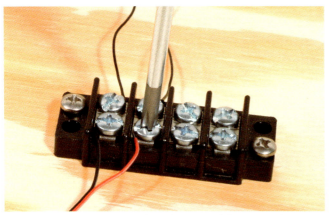

3. Attach additional wire to the other side of the terminals. Run this wire to your power pack and control panel location.

4. Lighted accessories like streetlights can operate on either AC or DC power. Connect the wires for accessories to the appropriate terminal on the back of your power pack.

5. As soon as you turn on the power pack, the light goes on. You can connect additional lights in the same manner.

Using a power distribution bus

A power distribution bus allows you to connect multiple accessories to the same set of power leads. Run the two power leads from your power pack to the underside of the layout. Tap into these power bus wires to connect the accessories. You can also use terminal strips to distribute power to accessories.

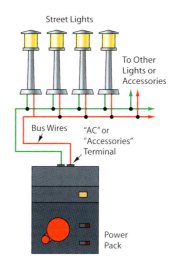

Wiring an On/Off switch

Accessories are fun, but there might be times when you don't want them to operate while you run your trains. In that case, you need to wire an On/Off switch into the circuit. You can use either an Atlas connector or a single-pole, single-throw toggle switch to turn accessories on and off. In this example, we'll use an Atlas connector.

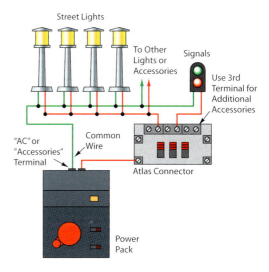

An Atlas connector turns track sections on and off, and it also works well to turn accessories on and off. To wire accessories through the connector, route one of the power leads from the power pack to a terminal on the connector.

On or off. When using an On/Off switch, you can use a common-wire return for powered accessories to minimize the amount of wire needed. Common-wire returns operate in the same way as common-rail block wiring. Connect one lead from each accessory to the same wire and connect this wire to one accessory terminal on your power pack. Then, connect the other accessory leads through On/Off switches so you can control the accessories you want to operate.

Wiring tips

CHAPTER **8**

When wiring your model railroad, it's always wise to follow one basic rule — keep it neat. There's nothing worse than trying to work underneath a layout in a mess of wires and connections, all tied together without any rules or patterns.

There are several tips and suggestions that can help you keep your wiring connections neat, orderly, and reliable. Let's take a look at a few of them.

Running wires

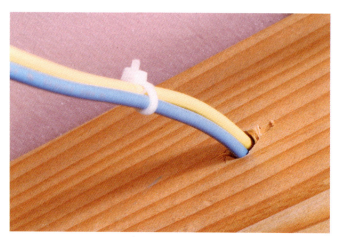

When running wires underneath your layout, run them in a common area. This allows you to group the wires and bundle them into neat cable assemblies. Use wire ties to bundle groups of wires. You can also drill holes in your benchwork to route wires along the underside of your table.

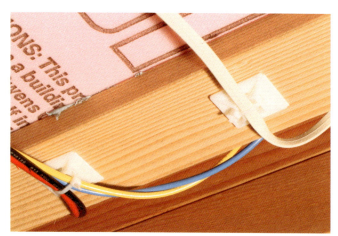

Wire fasteners allow you to attach wires to your benchwork. Wire fasteners come in different styles. Some attach to the benchwork with adhesive backing. Others mount to the benchwork with a wood screw.

Keeping it neat

Labeling wire connections

While you may know what each wire does right after you finish wiring your layout, you may not recall the function a year or two later when something stops working or you want to revise the configuration of your electrical connections.

As you make your electrical connections, label all wires and terminal strips so you can quickly and easily identify the function of each wire.

Be sure to use a name that is complete and clearly identifies the function of the particular wire. For instance, the label "switch machine" isn't really descriptive for a layout that has 15 or 20 motorized turnouts. Instead, give each connection a unique identifying label so you immediately know the function of the wire, such as "Junction Switch Machine."

Use logical label names

Suggested name	Wire function
Common	Common-rail feeder wire
Block 1, Block 2	Block feeder wires
(location) spur	Track spur feeder at specific location on your layout
Reverse loop	Reversing loop section feeder wires
Acc. power bus	Accessories power bus wires
(location) turnout	Turnout motor power leads to specific locations on your layout

No muss, no fuss

How would you like to troubleshoot an electrical problem in this rat's nest of wires? Many model railroaders wire their layouts in this fashion only to regret it when something stops working. Tracing a wiring problem on layouts that don't use neat wire bundles, color codes, and wire labels can be like searching for the proverbial needle in a haystack. While just running wires wherever they need to go can make for a quicker installation, at some point it will come back to haunt you.

You can label your wires in a number of ways. One of the easiest methods is to use a pen to mark the function of each wire right on the adjoining benchwork. This approach offers several benefits; the biggest one being that there are no tags to fall off. Remember, it doesn't have to be pretty, it just has to work.

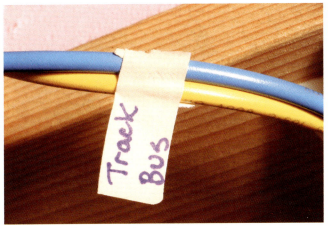

Adhesive labels also work for marking your wire connections. Buy adhesive-backed labels that allow enough space to mark the description. Peel the label from the backing and wrap it around the wire, placing the adhesive sides against each other.

Insulate those wires

Exposed wires are trouble waiting to happen. Even if bare wires appear to be in no danger of contacting other wires, the potential exists for problems down the road. A minor disturbance underneath the layout can lead to a sudden short circuit, bringing your trains to a screeching halt.

Whenever you strip wire insulation to make a wire splice or to tap into a bus wire, insulate the connection with electrical tape. Attach the end of the tape to one side of the joint. Wrap the tape tightly around the wire joint. Stretch the tape as you wrap it around the wire; this helps it adhere to the splice. Cut the tape from the roll when the joint is completely insulated.

Shrink tubing also works to insulate wire joints. It's quick and easy to use provided you have a heat gun. Remember to insert the tubing on the wire before you make the solder joint.

Alternatives to soldering wires

Splicing wires together works, but mechanical options also exist that provide secure, insulated connections. If need be, you can undo these connections with minimal effort.

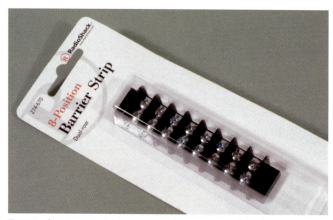

Terminal strips provide a convenient way to make wire connections. They allow you to fasten wires securely in place, yet you can easily remove them if you need to change your wiring configuration.

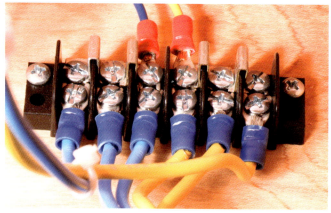

Bus bars connect all the terminal strip connections together. This comes in handy when you use terminal strips for power distribution. Install the bus bar on one side of the terminal strip and tighten all the screws. Attach accessory leads to the screws on the other side of the terminal strip.

Install the terminal strip to the underside of your benchwork using wood screws or short drywall screws. Attach the wires to the terminal strips as appropriate. You can place the bare wire under the screw connector or use a spade crimp connector. With either method, tighten the screw securely.

Push-in wire connectors allow you to attach wires without crimping or soldering. To use these connectors, you strip the insulation from the wires and insert them into the holes in the connector body. Clips inside hold the wires securely. These connectors tend to work better on solid-core wire.

Tap, or suitcase, connectors also work to join wires together. These connectors are handy for attaching track feeders to bus wires. To use, you place the connector over the main wire, allowing it to pass through the connector. Then, insert the feeder wire into the other slot. Use pliers to drive the metal clip into the wire insulation. Snap the cover closed when done to prevent short circuits.

Using splice connectors

Splice connectors allow you to join wires without solder or electrical tape. Insert one wire into the splice connector. Push the wire into the connector until it stops. Make sure all the wire conductor is covered by the connector's insulation.

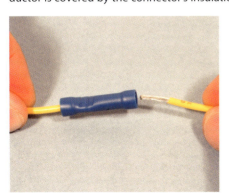

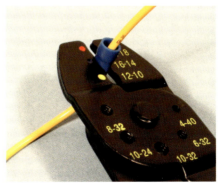

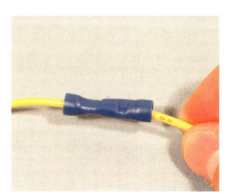

Crimp the connector in your wire crimp tool. Squeeze the connector so it collapses around the wire, holding it tight. Crimp the second wire in the tool. The result is a finished connection, ready for use.

Using crimp connectors

Crimp connectors allow you to add a mechanical fastener to the end of a wire. These connectors come in a variety of sizes and functions. They make it easy to install and remove wire connections.

Crimp connectors	
Connector color	**Wire size**
Red	18-22 Gauge
Blue	14-16 Gauge
Yellow	10-12 Gauge

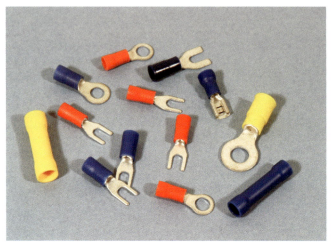

Crimp connectors are color coded based on wire size. Use the table to select the proper size connectors when shopping for supplies.

A spade connector is a commonly used type of crimp connector on model railroads. You can use this connector to securely attach wires to a terminal strip or to the screw terminals on a power pack. Spade connectors also allow you to remove the wires quickly should the need arise.

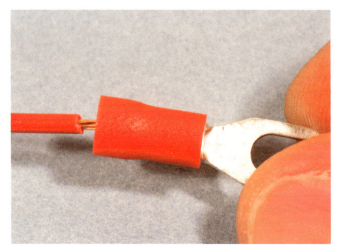

Crimp connectors are easy to use. Strip the insulation from the wire. Then insert the crimp connector on the end of the wire until the exposed conductor is inside the crimp connector insulation.

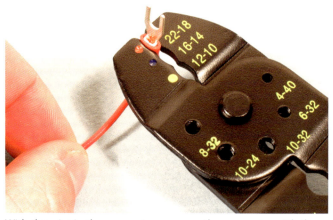

With the wire in the connector, squeeze the connector with the crimping tool. Afterwards, give the connector a gentle tug to make sure it's fastened to the wire.

Finding tools and materials

A hobby shop is a good source for the materials you'll need in wiring a layout, especially power packs, switch machines, and Atlas electrical components. If there's not a shop nearby, check the advertising in *Model Railroader* and the resources listed below. Mail-order electronics suppliers as well as some tool dealers carry wiring products.

However, you'll also need tools and materials that hobby shops don't stock. Here are some sources you should know:

RadioShack, the nationwide retail electronics chain, stocks tools, wire, switches, test equipment, and other components. If a local store doesn't have an item, you can order it at www.radioshack.com. The RadioShack catalog is also a useful reference.

Don't overlook hardware stores for wiring tools and materials, including soldering guns and solder, wire sized 22 AWG and larger, IDC connectors, cable ties, heat-shrink tubing, and many other handy items.

Newark InOne is a national supplier of wiring components, mainly for businesses but offers consumer sales through its Web site, www.newark.com.

Mouser Electronics is another national electronics supplier. Orders can be placed by telephone, 800-346-6873, fax or e-mail. You can view its Web site at www.mouser.com.

Check the telephone directory under Electronic Equipment & Supplies for nearby electrical or electronics suppliers. Even if there's not a retailer listed, many wholesalers will have retail sales counters. Often these suppliers publish catalogs of the lines they carry.

Suppliers and manufacturers

Aristo-Craft Trains
698 S. 21st St.
Irvington, NJ 07111
973-351-9800
www.aristocraft.com

Atlas Model Railroad
378 Florence Ave.
Hillside, NJ 07205
908-687-0880
www.atlasrr.com

Cir-Kit Concepts
32 Woodlake Dr. SE
Rochester, MN 55904
800-676-4252 or 507-288-0860
www.cir-kitconcepts.com

Circuitron
211 Rocbaar Dr.
Romeoville, IL 60446
815-886-9010

CVP Products
P.O. Box 835772
Richardson, TX 75083
972-238-9966
www.cvpusa.com

Dallee Electronics
246 W. Main St.
Leola, PA 17540
717-661-7041
www.dallee.com

Digitrax
450 Cemetery St. Suite 206
Norcross, GA 30071
770-441-7992
www.digitrax.com

ESU (LokSound)
Sales
PO Box 77
Upsala MN 56384
320-573-4300
www.loksound.com

GC/Waldom
1801 Morgan St.
Rockford, IL 61102
800-435-2931
gcwaldom.com

Hobby Surplus
PO Box 2170
New Britain, CT 06050
800-233-0872
www.hobbysurplus.com

Kadee Quality Products
673 Ave. C
White City, OR 97503
541-826-3883
www.kadee.com

Lenz Agency of North America (Lenz Elektronik)
PO Box 143
Chelmsford, MA 01824
978-250-1494
www.lenz.com

Micro-Mark
340 Snyder Ave.
Berkeley Heights, NJ 07922
800-225-1066
www.micromark.com

Miniatronics
561-K Acorn St.
Deer Park, NY 11729
800-942-9439
www.miniatronics.com

Model Rectifier Corp. (MRC)
80 Newfield Ave.
Edison, NJ 08837
732-225-2100
www.modelrectifier.com

National Model Railroad Association (NMRA)
4121 Cromwell Rd.
Chattanooga, TN 37421
423-892-2846
www.nmra.org

Micro-Trains Line
351 Rogue River Parkway
PO Box 1200
Talent, OR 97540
541-535-1755
www.micro-trains.com

North Coast Engineering
1900 Empire Blvd., Suite 303
Webster, NY 14580
716-671-0370
www.tttrains.com/northcoast

Plastruct
1020 S. Wallace Pl.
City of Industry, CA 91748
800-666-7015 or 626-912-7016
www.plastruct.com

Real Rail Effects
PO Box 1627
Highland, IN 46322
773-202-9931
www.tttrains.com/rre

Scale Shops
731 Vista Way
Prescott, AZ 86303
928-541-1373
www.scaleshops.com

Soundtraxx DCC
210 Rock Point Dr.
Durango, CO 81301
970-259-0690
www.soundtraxx.com

Tomar Industries
9520 E. Napier Ave.
Benton Harbor, MI 49022
877-697-9731
www.tomarindustries.com

Trout Creek Engineering (Classic Miniatures/Taurus Products)
12874 County Road 314 B
Buena Vista, CO 81211
719-395-8076
www.troutcreekeng.com

Start building your next layout!

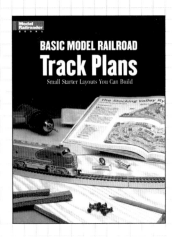

Basic Model Railroad Track Plans

From *Model Railroader*, these simple layout designs are ideal for beginners. Features full-color plans and construction techniques for HO and N scale starter layouts.

12237 • $16.95

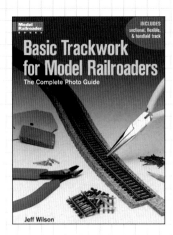

Basic Trackwork for Model Railroaders

Offers easy-to-follow techniques for installing sturdy trackwork, fitting the roadbed, laying track, and finishing with lineside details. Cover turnouts, cleaning and maintenance, and other special techniques.

12254 • $19.95

Maintaining & Repairing Your Scale Model Trains

With step-by-step instructions, photos, and illustrations, this book covers the basic techniques needed to maintain and repair DC-powered model locomotives, rolling stock, and layouts.

12210 • $17.95

Every issue includes intriguing articles that take you on a tour of the world's finest layouts and introduce you to the hobby's experts. You'll also discover a wealth of prototype data, detailed how-to instructions, product reviews, tips, techniques, and so much more!

12 issues per year

Basic Model Railroad Benchwork: The Complete Photo Guide

Step-by-step instructions and an illustrated teaching method take the mystery out of constructing model railroad benchwork. Covers the materials, tools, and basic skills required to make sturdy benchwork for any size or scale layout. By Jeff Wilson. 8¼ x 10¾; 96 pgs.; 250 color photos; 25 illustrations; softcover.

12241 • $18.95

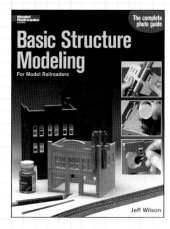

Basic Structure Modeling for Model Railroaders

Photo-driven projects demonstrate the tools, materials, and techniques used when modeling plastic or wooden structures. Offers techniques for realistic painting, weathering, detailing, and more.

12258 • $19.95